BRINGING
UP
BEAVER

Two Orphaned Beaver Kits,
Their Humans, and
Our Journey Back *to the* Wild

JOHN ABERTH

PEGASUS BOOKS
NEW YORK LONDON

BRINGING UP BEAVER

Pegasus Books, Ltd.
148 W 37th Street, 13th Floor
New York, NY 10018

First Pegasus Books edition August 2025

Interior design by Maria Fernandez

Library of Congress Cataloging-in-Publication Data is available.

ISBN: 978-1-63936-933-1

10 9 8 7 6 5 4 3 2 1

Printed in the United States of America
Distributed by Simon & Schuster
www.pegasusbooks.com

For BK

Contents

1: Beaver in the Bathtub   1

2: Walking My Beaver   25

3: Beaver in the Basement   45

4: The Mating Game   69

5: Stream Time   97

6: Second Winter   131

7: Back to the Wild   147

Postscript: The Tragedy of Trapping   169

The Aberth Manifesto: Six Ways to Coexist with Wild Animals   194

Acknowledgments   196

Index   197

1

Beaver in the Bathtub

I t was six o'clock in the evening on the second Sunday of May in the year 2020. I was just sitting down to dinner with my wife, Laura, when the phone rang.

"Hello? Is that John Aberth, the wildlife rehabber?"

I hesitated a second before answering. I've gotten some mighty strange calls over the nine years I've been practicing wildlife rehab. One time a woman called me at two o'clock in the morning, crying hysterically because she had run over a rat and wanted to know if I could save it. I told her, as gently as I could, that I didn't rehab rats but instead fed them to raptors—hawks, owls, and falcons—whom I was rehabbing and who needed free, easy meals. She hung up the phone.

The man currently on the phone sounded more reasonable. Josh was from St. Albans, Vermont, about eighty miles to the northwest of me, and said he had found a baby beaver while walking the rail trail—a walking trail that ran along a disused and disassembled railroad line—with his wife, Mayla. In truth, a call like this was not wholly unexpected. I began noticing an uptick in rehab calls beginning in March when we went into lockdown in Vermont due to the Coronavirus pandemic. People had more time on their hands and therefore began taking more walks and rambles, in the course of which they stumbled upon wildlife that needed rescuing. In Josh's case, his attention had been drawn to a little reddish-brown furry creature that made a sound eerily mimicking the cry of a human baby. He picked it up and immediately saw it was a beaver, the dead giveaway being its tail: flat, paddle-shaped, and scaly. He took it home and put it in a box with some sticks. Then he consulted the Vermont Department of Fish and Wildlife's web page and found their list of licensed wildlife rehabilitators. He called me because I listed beavers as one of the animals I had a "special interest" in rehabbing, along with raptors, mink, and weasels.

I was obligated to ask Josh the next question: How did he know the beaver was orphaned? Many "abandoned" baby animals are not really alone. Deer fawns, for example, are often left by their mothers for long periods while they forage for food—essential if does are to continue to nurse their young. Josh said a farmer who owned land next to the trail didn't want beavers flooding his property and had used a backhoe to take out their dam before crushing their lodge (both potentially illegal actions). The beaver kit was the only survivor of the colony. Satisfied, I arranged a time and place to meet for the handoff.

Beavers get a bad rap. If wildlife are the "persecuted minority" of the animal world—to whom almost no laws protecting against cruelty to animals apply—then beavers are the persecuted minority of wild animals. They are in the same family as rats. Most people consider them a nuisance. In truth, beavers are critically important to our local ecology—a keystone species. The wetland habitats they create have been compared to rainforests and coral reefs in terms of the biological diversity they support. Their ponds act as water storage and catchment areas to help mitigate droughts and floods, which can be of great benefit to farmers, like the one who had bulldozed this kit's lodge and family.

To be honest, I've always regarded beavers as really cool animals. Every birthday growing up, I "gifted" myself with beavers by going to our local beaver pond in the early dawn hours, when I knew they would be most active. There, I've not only seen beavers swimming around the pond, but also moose and deer wading through its shallows; mink scrambling along its banks; geese and ducks floating on its surface; kingfishers diving into its depths; and frogs, newts, and fish skimming over its bottom. All enjoy a feast of natural exchange that beaver dams make possible. The dams themselves are engineering marvels, masterpieces of mud and sticks. Moreover, beavers have been hailed in the news recently as "Climate Change Superheroes" because their ponds act as powerful carbon sinks that can help us fight global warming. Why do I rehab beavers? Because you save a beaver, and you save the world—a whole world of wildlife that thrives in a beaver-managed ecosystem unlike any other.

Nonetheless, I had to confess I had never had the opportunity to rehab a beaver before. Though I worked in wildlife rehab for years, it was a second career after retiring from teaching college-level history in 2011. But I have always been drawn to wild animals and alleviating their suffering and distress. As a boy, I remember how one day, my brother and his friend rescued a young hawk from the side of the road that was sitting on the ground, unable to fly. They brought it home and set it up in the back shed of the farmhouse, where it perched on the edge of a toolbox and hid its head under its wing, a sure sign of distress because it means the bird is attempting to conserve metabolic heat by going to sleep at the cost of vigilance against predators. The hawk died the next day. Now, I would know exactly what to do to save this bird from starvation.

After I got off the phone with Josh, Laura insisted I call someone more experienced to find out what I was in for. After some research on the internet, I found Cher. I'll call her the Beaver Lady. She was a renowned beaver rehabber in New York State with some thirty years of experience, a fountain of knowledge on all things beaver. In short, a godsend.

Beaver Lady told me everything I needed to know about rehabbing beavers. There was a lot to know! She told me, for example, that unlike other wildlife orphans, who can be released in a matter of weeks or months, orphaned baby beavers have to be raised by the rehabber for two whole years because that is how long they stay with their parents in the wild before dispersing on their own. Despite being furbearing mammals, beavers are basically aquatic in nature and therefore need to be swum in some body of water at least four times a day. This is because they not only poop and pee only in water, but also drink a lot of water—essential for their digestion—and regard water as their safe space.

Finally, Beaver Lady told me that, whereas other orphaned animals require just three things from the rehabber—food, warmth, and shelter—baby beavers need a fourth thing—companionship. Beavers, she explained, are very social animals: They mate for life and form close bonds within their family or colony. Now, we were to be this beaver's family, and therefore Laura and I had to form those bonds, too. If we didn't, the beaver would die from loneliness. Beaver Lady said that she had seen it happen with kits passed from rehabber to rehabber, leaving the beavers unsettled and depressed. In fact, Beaver Lady said, nine out of ten beaver kits in rehab die, often due to "rehabber error." Although becoming attached to a beaver went against my instincts as a rehabber (i.e., to keep patients "wild") I was also determined to beat the odds and keep my beaver alive. Moreover, Beaver Lady assured me that parental bonding is vital and beaver kits "wild up" soon after being released after their second year.

All this, Beaver Lady said, make beavers the most difficult of all wild animals to rehab.

But also the most rewarding.

When I hung up the phone, I gave the news to Laura.

"Two years?! It's like we're getting a child! A real-life beaver-child!"

It was true. It was a big commitment, including for Laura, who would have to help me care for this baby beaver. It was like we were having our first child together. Indeed, we'd be doing many of the same things one does for a human child: bottle feeding, bathing, cuddling, putting down for naps. At least we wouldn't be changing diapers. But we were probably going to have some sleepless nights.

We've never had kids of our own, nor did we want to. We had our hands full with thirteen horses and a cat. But having kids also never seemed to be part of our DNA. I was infertile. We saw how much my brother and his wife went through in order to adopt. Being responsible for another's life seemed to be asking to give up too much of ourselves. A friend of mine, who had three kids of his own, once told me I was "incomplete" for not having kids. But I certainly didn't feel that way. What I could not predict, however, was how much this baby beaver would trigger some hidden maternal instinct in Laura and a paternal instinct in me. In one of life's mysterious but wonderful twists, she and I came to care for and, yes, love this wild animal, almost as if it were our own child.

When I brought the beaver home, the first thing I did was weigh him. He weighed in at just one and a half pounds, which meant he was only about a week old. He was so small he could almost fit in the palm of my hand. He also made a noise—"aaaya, aaaya"—that Laura said sounded like a human baby and tugged at her heartstrings. After debating whether to give the beaver a name, Laura and I began calling him "BK," short for Beaver Kit.

Our first task was to make a home for BK. This was easily solved: He would live in our bathtub, since where else in the house could he have such ready access to water? I fashioned a small house for BK by putting a hard blue plastic box tipped over on its side into one end of the tub. I replaced the plastic box with a wooden one as soon as BK became mouthy, chewing everything in sight. Into the house I put a heating pad warmed in the microwave, covered with a scrap of mink fur. I hoped the fur-covered heating pad might approximate a beaver mother's warm belly, and perhaps make BK feel a little more at home.

The fur came from someone who had donated all her grandmother's fur coats to be used in wildlife rehab. No longer heirlooms of prestige, the fur coats had become badges of cruelty—trapping animals so they could be skinned into fur pelts—that their current owner wouldn't be caught dead wearing. It was poetic justice that these coats of death were to be cut into scraps that would help give life to newborn wildlife. This was especially apropos for beavers, seeing as how they were—and still are—trapped ceaselessly for their fur during the insatiable pelt trade that accompanied European settlers' "discovery" of the New World. To complete the welcome, I also placed a Beaver Buddy into the house. This was a furry beaver toy that could offer BK a little companionship, at least when I was not around.

Our next task was a bigger one: to find a way to feed BK. If we couldn't figure this out, BK would never be able to grow or even survive. I found a powdered milk formula that was specially formulated for beavers—composed of 50 percent fat and 30 percent protein—which I dissolved in water and tried to bottle-feed BK. But he kept pushing away the nipple. Laura and I were beginning to panic. BK simply wouldn't eat! Were we feeding him wrong? Did he not like the formula? Is this what all parents of newborns go through?!

It was time to call Beaver Lady again. Cher suggested I instead use a canula-tipped syringe. It worked! The syringe allowed me to more easily and precisely introduce milk into BK's mouth. Once he got a taste of the milk, BK started sucking on his own. By the third day, BK figured out how to essentially feed himself. He'd grab the syringe with his Sasquatch-like paws and simply suck on the canula so hard that the plunger moved by itself. Neither I nor Laura had to hold it at all! All we had to do was refill the syringe as quickly as we could when BK sucked it dry and cried for more. We were so proud of BK (and so relieved)! Laura said it showed an independent streak, that BK liked to do things for himself. She posed with BK on her lap, holding her hands out as if to say, "Look Ma, I can feed my baby beaver with no hands!" Pretty soon, BK was guzzling down about eight ounces, or one cup, of milk a day.

By the fourth week of his life, BK began transitioning to solid food. Laura and I would bring him poplar and willow sticks, just like his older beaver siblings would have done in the wild. But we also gave him Rodent Chow—a special dietary supplement in pellet or nugget form that BK liked to chew on. In spite of our relief and gratitude for how well BK was able to feed himself, there was also something about his feeding habits that revolted us: BK would eat his own poo! This was almost certainly not something parents of a human child would have to deal with. But coprophagia is quite common in the animal world. BK would sit on his tail in shallow water and then bend over to pull poo balls out of his butt and eat them. I researched coprophagia and found it was actually a good thing. It allowed BK to extract extra nutrients from the woody matter he'd eaten the first time around, which had been processed as it passed through his digestive system and could now be utilized.

At least four times a day, including after every feeding, Laura and I swam BK. Initially this was done in the bathtub, where BK lived for the first two and a half months of his life. But the bathtub was rather small and didn't give BK much room for swimming. We figured out a better alternative, which was to have BK swim in an outdoor pool, jury-rigged from a plastic kidney-shaped pool originally meant as an ornament for gardens. I set up the pool behind the house, where I could fill it up with warm water piped directly from the hot water tank through a hose snaked out of a window in the basement. BK preferred to swim in lukewarm water, which mimicked how beaver kits in the wild swim out from the lodge to the shallow end of the pond, where the water is warmer. Here, Laura and I could supervise BK's swimming, like any good parents would do for their child.

Only BK did not really need supervising. He was already a great swimmer! I came to appreciate just how well-adapted BK's body was for an aquatic environment. For starters, there were his hind feet, which had webbing between the toes, turning them into flippers with which BK could easily propel himself through the water.

Then there was his tail, which acted as a rudder-cum-keel, keeping him right-side-up and steady in the water while also allowing him to change direction on a dime. I watched BK do 360-degree "wheelies" in the water, which he seemed to do just for fun. Finally, BK's eyes, ears, and nose were also extraordinarily well-adapted for water. Whenever BK dived, his ears and nostrils would automatically close so no water would enter, while a translucent "nictating" membrane—the so-called third eyelid—would come across each eye to protect it, like built-in goggles. Birds and reptiles also have nictating membranes, and with BK, they turned his eyes bluish underwater. All this made BK as graceful in the water as he was awkward on land, which he was to demonstrate later.

The other great advantage of the outdoor pool was that I did not have to drain and then fill it up after every use, as I had to do with the bathtub. I could simply let the water sit and then refresh it with a little more water from the hot water tank whenever BK had to swim again, provided I fished out BK's poo, which BK always made at the beginning of every swim. Monitoring BK's poo was another thing Laura and I obsessed over as surrogate beaver parents: The condition of the poo reflected the condition of BK's gut and overall health. In the first few weeks, BK's poo was typically a milky tan color that sank to the bottom of the pool and had the consistency of sticky mud. Obviously, this was a by-product of BK's strong appetite for milk. But by the fourth week, when BK started eating more woody matter, his poo became a dark brown and floated to the surface, making it easier for me to scoop out. BK also occasionally had diarrhea at this time, which greatly alarmed us. I called Beaver Lady and she assured me this was normal as his body adjusted to a changing diet.

But the days when BK had projectile diarrhea—akin to projectile vomiting but perhaps even more disgusting—were not fun. One particularly bad incident happened on the last day of May, when BK was about a month old. He had been having diarrhea all day—very watery with grayish bits floating in it. We swam him in the bathtub because it was important on days like this that BK drink lots of water. When Laura picked him up to towel off, suddenly BK exploded diarrhea all over the place: on the floor, on the walls, on Laura's computer, and, of course, on Laura herself. She may even have gotten some in her mouth, because she complained of a nutty aftertaste! The next morning, however, BK's poo was back to normal. He did a small solid tan poo in the bathtub that sank, followed by a second, larger poo that was a darker tan-brown and floated because it contained more woody fiber. Laura and I breathed a big sigh of relief.

The greatest advantage of the outdoor pool was that there, BK could splash and make a mess as much as he wanted, because it was all outside. I should note that, with the pool outside constantly filled with water, it became attractive to other denizens of the wild. One day BK and I came out to find a big green bullfrog hiding among all the willow greenery Laura had put in for BK to chew on. BK didn't seem to mind the frog; they mostly kept out of each other's way. Except one day, BK came face to face with Mrs. Frog, sniffing her out before she jumped hastily out of the way. The next day, Mrs. Frog was gone, but she left behind what looked like eggs along the side of the pool, although I never saw them hatch into tadpoles.

After every swim, which kept getting longer and longer, BK groomed himself. First, he rubbed his face and head with his forepaws. Then he scratched himself underneath his arms with his large hind feet, first under one arm, then under the other, while holding out his arm with his paw clenched into a fist. Finally, he sat on his tail with his belly bowed out like a Buddha, rubbing and scratching all over. Sometimes, when he scratched himself under his chin, he would bare his impressive orange-colored incisors. (The orange color comes from the iron in beavers' teeth that makes them so strong.)

This scratching ritual had a specific purpose: not just to clean the fur, but also to keep it *oiled*. BK would secrete an oily substance from his butt called castoreum, which he'd collect while bent over in his Buddha pose. BK would then spread this oil all over his fur to help keep it waterproof. Sometimes I'd help BK by combing his fur, especially on the top side of his body where he could not reach, using a fine-tooth flea comb. In this way, I got to know beaver fur intimately. BK had two kinds of fur: a dark, dense layer lying close to the skin that had fine hairs; then a lighter, more reddish fur on top with longer strands that felt coarser and flared out from the body, making BK look bigger than he was. Together, these two layers of fur trapped air and made for a kind of insulation that kept BK warm as he swam in cold water. But it was also a once-valuable fur that killed beavers, trapped to the point of near extinction for pelts used to make felt hats that were all the rage in men's fashion from the sixteenth to the nineteenth centuries. BK's tail, on the other hand, felt cool and dry, just like a snake's skin, and was scaly. In the Middle Ages, the Catholic Church allowed people to eat beaver tails during Lent because they classified it as a kind of fish, owing to its scaly appearance.

After his swim and groom, BK was allowed to wander on the lawn to dry himself off. At first, he'd look like a drowned rat, but after five or ten minutes, he'd poof out again and be back to his furry self. Sometimes Laura or I would walk or run around the lawn in front of BK and he'd follow us like a puppy. BK had two gaits: a waddle, in which he'd walk in four beats with his belly swinging ponderously from side to side; and a "galumph," in which he would gallop in two beats, his hind and fore legs each moving together as a pair, when he wanted to move faster and keep up with us. At the end of nearly every one of these exercise sessions, BK would let out a great yawn!

Finally, there was companionship. Laura and I tried to make BK feel he was family by spending quality time with him. (This was made easier by the fact that, due to the lockdown imposed by the Coronavirus pandemic, I was furloughed from my part-time job as a school bus driver.) Of course, this BK Time was in addition to the time Laura and I spent feeding and bathing him, whether in the bathtub or in the outdoor pool. These activities punctuated our quality BK Time. Even if Laura or I simply had to go to the bathroom, it was BK Time, and he was right there, poking his head above the rim of the bathtub. If either of us wanted to take a shower, we had to take BK's house out of the bathtub, with BK inside it, and deposit both on the bathroom floor. We could then do our business while keeping a wet eye on BK as he wandered around the bathroom.

This was somewhat risky as our entire bathroom, including the floor, was made of wood and now within easy reach of BK's mouth. Yet BK never bothered the wood since he had far more interesting items to engage his attention. These included our smelly socks, underwear, shirts, and pants, which we had deposited on the floor before getting in the shower. BK loved to sniff, chew, and shake them in his mouth, or fling them across the floor and drag them into his house for hoarding! Sometimes we'd reach out of the shower and play a little tug-of-war with BK over our clothes, or watch BK galumph around the bathroom floor like one of our horses free lunging around the indoor riding arena. Otherwise, BK was content to scratch or groom himself or play with his Beaver Buddy, which by this stage was becoming rather ragged and chewed up. BK also had an assortment of toys to play with, such as glitter balls and, yes, sticks that Laura and I would roll or toss across the floor for BK to chase after and fetch.

It was during these play sessions that we came to appreciate BK's best sense—smell. After all, this was how BK recognized us, which showed how important it was. This was why, for example, he loved to play with our smelly clothes. And it was why he'd hiss at any strangers—even if they were close relatives, such as Laura's brother—who happened to come over; it showed that BK had attached himself to us and only us, and not just to any human. BK would even hiss at us if we'd just gotten out of the shower because he couldn't recognize our clean scent. A beaver's hiss is really quite alarming: It's deep and menacing and sounds like Darth Vader! When BK wanted something from us, on the other hand, he'd make his human-like baby cry—"aaaya, aaaya"—that was nearly impossible to ignore. This meant either Laura or I would sometimes have to get up at two or three o'clock in the morning to feed BK. For, like any hungry infant, BK would insistently cry for us—only in this instance, from the bathtub—and he would not stop until he got what he wanted!

As the days became longer and more pleasant in June and July, we spent more time outside with BK. When BK wasn't playing with Beaver Buddy, Laura and I would get him to play a game: I would sit at one end of the lawn and Laura at the other, and we'd take turns calling BK. It was pretty clear that BK couldn't see us, as beavers have terrible eyesight. But he could hear us, and we'd each call to him and pat the ground, creating tremors BK seemed to feel. After he'd come galumphing over to one or the other of us, we'd reward BK with a pat or stroke of his fur, and maybe a Rodent Chow nugget.

Even though BK would come when called, he could never be left unattended. This was because a small stream ran not fifty feet behind our house, and the gurgling sound of its flowing waters acted as a siren song to BK, calling him to come dam it up! Often, he would stand on his hind feet and listen, particularly if he was in the tall grass where the lawn and the forest met. This was the signal that playtime was over and it was time to take BK back inside. I knew BK belonged in the wild, and he'd get there eventually. But in the meantime, he had a lot of growing up to do.

One day in early June, Laura and I were lounging with BK outside on the lawn when a thunderstorm blew in. There was a loud "boom!" and BK ran for shelter—not to his house, which was on the grass, but to us—just underneath my crotch, to be precise, where he cowered between my legs. A wonderful and unexpected wave of protective, paternal feeling washed over me like never before. BK had accepted me as his surrogate parent, and I realized for the first time that I was truly a parent to BK. I was his first refuge from danger. I found that I cared deeply for BK and wanted him not just to be safe, but to *feel* safe and secure. There were plenty of other ways in which BK showed his implicit trust in me—like the way he allowed himself to fall asleep in the crook of my arm, dreaming his beaver dreams; or the way he bared his belly, the most vulnerable part of his body, to me as he lay upside down playing with Beaver Buddy; or the way he reached for my hand when he first emerged, wet and disheveled, from swimming in the outdoor pool. BK and I had bonded.

By mid-July, BK was a full ten pounds and outgrowing his house, the bathtub, and even my lap! It was getting time to move him to the outdoor enclosure behind our house. But first, its current occupant had to be released.

On BK's third day with us, he was joined in the bathroom—the warmest room in the house—by an owlet, an orphaned owl, that had been found on the ground on the TAM (Trail Around Middlebury). The owl still had lots of down, meaning it was a nestling that had somehow gotten out of its nest and was unable to fly. I knew it was not a barred owl, our most common kind of owl, because two yellow, unblinking eyes stared up at me on either side of a large beak, all nestled within what looked like dirty gray cotton balls. Moreover, the owlet had two fuzzy little ear tufts, or "horns," starting on the top of its head. Barred owls always have brown eyes and no horns. That it was an owl, there was no doubt, as the bird turned its head 180 degrees (i.e., with its back facing me) to get a good look at me. Owls can do that because their skulls are not attached directly to their backbones.

Once I had settled the owlet into a makeshift nest, it soon started making "cheep, cheep" noises, meaning it was hungry! At first I fed the bird "pinkie" mice, baby mice that were almost pure meat and easily digestible. But later in the day I found a cough pellet, which all raptors cough up since they can't digest the bones and fur of their prey. So I knew the owlet's parents had fed her whole mice before she was orphaned. I then fed her "fuzzies," or little furry mice, in order to transition her to more normal food. I got all my mice—shipped frozen in varying sizes—from a rodent supply company, patronized not only by rehabbers but also by owners of mice-eating pets, such as snakes, lizards, and imprinted birds of prey flown by falconers. I kept all these frozen mice in a dedicated chest freezer downstairs in the basement, for which Laura was grateful because it meant she didn't have to see dead mice every time she opened the fridge!

Throughout this process, I employed an "imprinting protocol," which meant I covered my face and hands so the bird did not associate humans with food. With raptors and corvids (i.e., crows and ravens), such a protocol is necessary if the birds are to be safely released back into the wild. Every time I fed the owlet, I wore a leather mask with a pointed beak over the nose to resemble a bird's beak. I also wore blue gloves over my hands and used forceps to insert the mice into the nestling's mouth.

The owlet grew a lot faster than BK. Just ten days after she came to me, the owlet's pin feathers emerged, and about twenty days after that, by mid-June, she had come into her adult plumage. In the meantime, I had moved her to the outdoor enclosure behind our house. The enclosure was twelve feet long by eight feet wide by eight feet high, with wooden slats on the inside so birds could not hurt their feet on the wire mesh that covered the ceiling and one wall looking out onto the forest. After her adult plumage came in, the owl began flying around the enclosure, trying out her flight feathers. I could also now identify her.

She was a long-eared owl, the dead giveaway being, of course, her long "horns," or ear tufts, although I noticed her right horn was growing faster than her left. (Was she "right-horned?!") But there were other indicators, such as her mottled brown plumage; her soft, high-pitched mewling noises that sounded something like a cat's meow, or "jaiow, jaiow" (hence the nickname "cat owl"); and the fact that she stretched up tall and thin whenever I came into the enclosure, typical behavior of long-eared owls, who are known for camouflaging themselves against tree trunks. By this time, the owl weighed in at nearly three hundred grams, on the heavier side for long-eared owls, indicating the owl was a female.

I no longer had to wear a mask and gloves when around the owl because she was now self-feeding, eating on her own the mice I put out for her. The owl was also flying well, circling around me whenever I came into the enclosure. But the last test the owl had to pass before being released was a "live prey test," in which the owl had to catch and kill live mice, a skill she would need to survive in the wild. This involved me capturing several live mice in a small Havahart trap, hobbling them, putting them on the shelf next to where the owl was perching, and seeing what she would do. Initially the owl simply watched the mice crawl around, but eventually she went after the mice, plucked them up in her talons, and pecked at them until they were dead. She then ate the mice by tearing off bits of their flesh, starting with their heads. Apparently the brain was the tastiest organ.

On July 14, the owl was released. I picked that day because the weather was fair and mid-July was when long-eared owls typically fledged, or left the nest. I found a site in Hinesburg, Vermont, for the owl's release, as it was on the western side of the state, in the vicinity of where the owl had originally been found, and where a number of long-eared owls had been sighted by bird-watchers. The site consisted of wide-open farm fields bordered by forest, a habitat favored by long-eared owls because they hunt in fields and nest in forests.

We left home with the owl at six o'clock in the afternoon. It took an hour to get to Hinesburg, so by the time we got to the release site, it was approaching dusk. This is the ideal time to release owls as they are more active at night. The owl had had a last meal of three mice during the day, so she should have been well-fed for her release. I wanted to give her as much of a head start as possible.

During the whole ride to Hinesburg, the owl was quiet in the carrier. When Laura and I got to the release site, I took the owl out to a field stretching to the east with a forest to the west that advanced toward the road within easy flying distance. I opened the carrier and set it on the ground. The owl would not come out, but rattled around inside the carrier. I scooped her out with my gloved hand, and the owl flew low a short distance to the east to a mowed part of the field. Immediately a flock of swallows came out of nowhere and dive-bombed the owl, like Messerschmitt Bf 109s swarming an enemy target! The owl took off, flying high this time, west toward the forest and the cover of the trees, getting great lift from her strong wings. She was flying high and fast now, escaping the pursuing swallows. Soon she was lost to sight. Although I had not bonded with the owl like I was doing with BK, I felt a great sense of exhilaration as I watched her fly off. She was free now, a fully wild bird. I picked up the carrier, and Laura and I headed home, back to BK.

2

Walking My Beaver

J ust four days after I released the long-eared owl, I moved BK out of the bathtub into his new digs. He now had a new house—a spacious Dogloo—and his old garden pool, now equipped with a wooden ramp I had specially made for him that allowed BK to come and go as he pleased. By no means had this been an easy move; it took some doing.

Preparations began nearly a month before the move itself. The first thing Laura and I had to teach BK was how to get in and out of the pool by himself. This was essential if BK was to have ready access to water for both drinking and pooing.

Laura and I started BK's training with a simple exercise: Could he get *out* of the pool on his own, once he was done swimming? We set up a simple ramp by leaning a wide board on the end of the pool where there was a sun shelf BK could use to haul himself onto the ramp. Then we covered the ramp with some astroturf I had purchased for the enclosure. An excess swatch of astroturf was allowed to hang into the water and cover one of the sun shelves. Sure enough, BK was able to get purchase on the astroturf and pull himself onto the ramp then clamber to the ground. Laura and I repeated this exercise a couple more times before moving to the next stage, which was to get BK to go *up* the ramp and then down into the pool.

For this next stage, we jury-rigged a two-stage ramp: A long board led up to the pool from the ground, and then a shorter board led into the water. Laura salvaged the short board from a rope swing, with the rope still attached. We threaded the rope through holes at one end of the board then up and over to the holes at the other end. This made for a kind of rope railing that BK could grab as he navigated his way down into the water, although BK seemed more interested in chewing on the rope! The excess rope at the other end was used to tie the short board to the long one going up to the pool. Laura and I introduced BK to the ramp the next time we brought him outside.

BK took to the ramp right away. He seemed to view it as a kind of game. He'd clamber up the long ramp, perch at the top for a bit, pausing either to chew on the rope, groom himself, or have a pee, and then scramble down the rope swing before belly flopping into the water with a splash!

After a while he'd clamber back out of the pool onto the rope swing board and then down the long ramp to the soft green grass. BK would do this multiple times in one session—as many as four—before tiring of the game. At first I spotted BK the whole way up and down the ramp, afraid he might fall off the edge onto the ground. But soon BK got so good at this game that I didn't have to worry. BK had it covered.

I made one last improvement to the ramp before putting it and the pool into the enclosure. I made it a three-stage ramp: one board going up, a second board going straight across the lip of the pool, so BK could have a platform to groom or pee, and a third board going down into the pool itself (the rope swing having been scrapped altogether). I attached the boards to each other by hinges so I could easily remove and fold the ramp whenever I had to dump the water in the pool and refill it (which I had to do every day because of BK's muddy feet!). I added wooden slats spaced four to five inches apart onto the first and third boards so BK would have traction even when the boards were wet. BK seemed very happy with my ramp. Laura said this was because BK liked being able to do things for himself, just like when he drank milk on his own from the syringe by sucking up the plunger.

Speaking of which, BK weaned himself off milk soon after he moved into the enclosure. He was now on a straight diet of willow and poplar sticks and Rodent Chow nuggets. I was relieved, because it was a lot easier to give BK sticks and nuggets than milk. The nuggets I ordered from Mazuri, a company that manufactured food for exotic pets and zoo animals. The sticks I got from Heidi, the Flower Girl. She ran a flower farm across the valley from us, cultivating fields of flowers that turned her hillside into a paradise every spring. But she also had over a hundred different varieties of willow, which constantly needed pruning. BK was undoubtedly the luckiest beaver in North America!

One final thing I had to do before moving BK was beaver-proof the enclosure. This involved stapling (with big metal staples pounded in with a hammer) half-inch wire mesh all the way around the inside to protect the wooden slats and support beams from being chewed. The wire mesh was coated with plastic so BK couldn't hurt his paws on the metal, and it was over three feet tall to protect the wood even when BK stood up on his hind legs. I also hosed down the entire enclosure to make sure it was clean.

Another lifestyle change BK had to get used to was living in a new house. Admittedly, this was not such a hardship: BK's new house was a spacious Dogloo, whose shape approximated that of a beaver lodge. The Dogloo even had a vent hole at the top, just as a beaver lodge would. I had found the Dogloo for free, being given away on somebody's lawn. After a thorough cleaning, it was time to introduce BK to his new home. Laura and I brought him out onto the lawn in his original blue plastic house, since it was so much lighter than the wooden one, and put it next to the Dogloo. BK stood by his old house for a while before going to investigate the Dogloo. He seemed to like it. BK liked the Dogloo even more when we put in a nice big comfy dog bed. On BK's first night out in the enclosure, I put in his old wooden house because it still had BK's smell, and something familiar might give him comfort in his strange new surroundings. BK immediately went into his old house and spent the night there, even though he could barely fit inside it.

About a week after BK had moved into the enclosure, we got an opportunity to positively identify the sex of BK. Male and female beavers look exactly the same. Their sexual organs are all internal, located within the cloaca. There are only two ways to tell a beaver's sex: by x-raying the beaver's abdomen, or by having the beaver excrete castoreum. If the beaver is a male, his baculum or penis bone (os penis) will show up on the x-ray; if the beaver is a female, there'll be nothing. However, the x-ray must be taken from the front, over the beaver's belly, because otherwise the spinal cord can obscure the os penis and one will falsely assume the beaver is a female. The other method is to get the beaver to excrete castoreum by pressing on its anus. Castoreum is an oily, orangey-brown liquid beavers secrete to groom their fur and mark their territory. The darker the castoreum, or the more it smells like motor oil, the more likely the beaver is to be a male. However, I had no idea what motor oil smelled like, and there was no way in hell I was going to squeeze BK's anus and smell his butt juice!

Instead Laura and I had our horse vet come with his portable machine to take an x-ray of BK. Laura put on a lead apron and held BK in her lap like a baby, with the x-ray plate behind BK as she held him with his stomach facing out. After squirming for a bit, BK finally gave in and calmly accepted being held with his belly exposed, a vulnerable position for any animal. The vet took a number of x-rays with his portable machine, which had issues powering up but eventually produced a number of images. After examining them, we determined BK was a male! His os penis showed up as a small slender bone dangling just underneath the third digit of BK's left hind foot, which he was holding higher than his right.

But perhaps the biggest change was BK's new routine, which was that Laura or I would walk BK out to the stream just behind our house, not fifty feet away from the enclosure. We usually let BK sleep in until mid-morning, lolling in his Dogloo on his waterproof dog bed. As soon as I opened the enclosure door, BK climbed out and made a beeline to the water, using the same trail every day. While Laura or I chaperoned, the other stayed behind to change the water in the outdoor pool, which was usually quite dirty from the day before. Then BK was taken to the stream again around noon and once more in the afternoon, for a total of three stream visits before we tucked him in for the night.

People often asked me if I worried that BK would simply wander off on his own during these excursions. I wasn't worried, for two reasons. First, BK never moved fast enough (at least on land) that Laura or I couldn't catch up with him. Second, BK was family. Just as people walk their dogs off-leash, I was confident BK would not stray far from those who gave him food, shelter, and, yes, love. But we always brought Beaver Buddy and some Rodent Chow nuggets to help entice BK out of the stream when it was time to go home.

The water we walked BK to was a little creek, barely a foot deep, that fed into the Flint Brook, which ran on the northeast side of our house and flowed all the way down into the valley, where it joined the Third Branch of the White River, which eventually flowed into the Connecticut River on the Vermont–New Hampshire border. Just behind our house, the creek widened into an inlet or cove about the size of BK's outdoor pool. Moreover, it cut into a bank under some tree roots where BK could play hide-and-seek and generally have fun exploring a natural environment.

It was my hope that during Stream Time, BK would learn some beaver life skills—such as how to build a dam or, more simply, how mud and sticks mold together—so he could survive when released into the wild. Indeed, BK spent more and more time in the stream as the summer wore on. While I sat on the bank and read a magazine or watched, BK explored the cove, diving among the tree roots lining the eastern bank and popping up somewhere else entirely, having found an underwater passage to his new location. Or he simply emerged from under the bank, triumphantly carrying an old waterlogged stick he had found, which he either chewed or added to a growing pile of like-minded sticks on a little sandbar in the middle of the stream. BK also had his pick of live green branches overhanging the stream to reach and chew on. To make the cove deeper, Laura started a small dam, across the downstream side, made out of river stones. Occasionally BK would help by pushing sticks, mud, or small rocks with his snout and forepaws onto the dam.

Proof that the dam was working was Mr. Trout. He was a fish that shared the cove with BK. Initially Mr. Trout was no more than a minnow. But in the past few weeks, I noticed Mr. Trout had grown bigger—more fish-sized—as the pool had gotten deeper. This proved that trout can greatly benefit from beaver habitat, since this habitat improves a pond's water quality, oxygen levels, and food resources as the water gets deeper and colder. One day BK met Mr. Trout face to face. When Mr. Trout touched

BK's foot, BK made a big splash with his tail and swam the other way!

The cove was still shallow enough for Laura and me to wade in on hot summer days and play with BK. BK was as playful as an otter: He would do 360-degree rolls and somersaults in the water, while Laura or I splashed him with our feet and tickled his tummy. We'd also play Beaver Wrestle, using Beaver Buddy to try to push BK backward as he swam and thrashed in the water. Sometimes, though, BK would simply reach up and hold my hand as I sat on a log stretching over the cove.

Eventually BK outgrew the cove, and it could no longer contain him. Beginning in the third week of August, BK decided to go exploring. At first he tried to explore downstream, but Laura and I wouldn't let him pass. That way led to the mighty Flint Brook and much more water and danger. We preferred he explore upstream, where the water was more placid. A downed tree formed a natural log dam on most of the upstream side of the cove, preventing BK from going farther. Until one day when BK popped his head up through the log's old roots on the eastern end of the cove, which BK was able to access from underneath the cove's eastern bank. Soon BK hauled his *whole body* up through the gap and waddled the short distance to the water on the other side of the dam.

There, the stream widened to a broad Swimway, ten feet wide from bank to bank and at least thirty feet long, from the log dam on the cove side to another log dam farther upstream. This other log dam was sufficient to contain BK for a while until somehow he figured out a way to go underneath that one as well. Laura and I had to make sure BK didn't go exploring farther upstream, because it led to a tangle of underbrush from which we'd never extricate BK. Mostly, though, BK was content to swim laps back and forth in this wide part of the stream. BK even started pushing mud around with his snout in an apparent attempt to make the Swimway deeper. A wide grassy sward on the eastern bank of the Swimway was perfect for Laura and me to set up folding chairs and supervise BK's swimming. This became BK's favorite part of the stream, so much so that I began calling his former swimming hole the Auld Cove. This was an homage to Aulds Cove in Nova Scotia, the last stop on the mainland before crossing the Canso Causeway to Cape Breton Island, where Laura and I used to vacation every summer at her family's oceanfront campground at Inverness.

Occasionally BK would come out of the water of his own accord to sit in my lap or Laura's for a wet cuddle, or else to nibble on my shoelaces. But most of all, BK wanted to play his favorite game, Beaver Wrestle. This was played with a towel twisted tightly into a roll, with BK grabbing onto the towel and pushing against it. I first played this game with BK when he was still living in the bathroom, and he never grew out of it. It was basically a pushing game, unlike tug-of-war, which is a pulling contest. In the wild, beaver kits play this game with each other. I had seen videos rehabbers took of orphaned beaver kit siblings wrestling. Like sumo wrestlers, the beaver kits would stand up on their hind legs and then grab onto each other, trying to push the other back as far as they would go. There was no real aggression to the wrestling; it was just a game to see who could push the hardest. I tried to mimic this as much as possible by pushing back against BK through the towel roll, and I made sure to let him win once in a while.

I often wondered why beavers love to wrestle. I assumed there was more to it than just fun. My theory was that they were building their upper body strength, the better to push trees over after chewing through their trunks. After all, I had seen some mighty big trees felled by beavers!

When it was time to bring BK in, Laura and I lured him onto land by teasing him with Beaver Buddy or with a bribe of Rodent Chow nuggets. But BK was getting wise to these ruses. Sometimes I simply had to grab him out of the Swimway or the Auld Cove, but BK was slippery! It was like trying to grab a big wet furry fish. I had to make sure BK's tail was tucked underneath him; otherwise, he pooed all over me. Even so, I always came back with wet pants! I was grateful on the days BK offered to walk back to the enclosure on his own.

In August, I entered into battle with a chipmunk who was trying to muscle in on BK's territory—namely, his enclosure. I first encountered Mr. Chipmunk when I tried to roust him out of the secondary entrance of the enclosure. This was a small, screened-in area attached to the main entrance designed to keep animals contained that happened to slip out the front door. Only, instead of running outside, Mr. Chipmunk ran into the enclosure with BK! This happened again and again. Why was Mr. Chipmunk so interested in BK's enclosure?

I soon discovered that Mr. Chipmunk wanted BK's Rodent Chow nuggets. After all, he was in the same biological family as BK, and if BK loved his nuggets, then so did Mr. Chipmunk! This was confirmed one day when I took BK down to the stream, leaving the door open and nuggets in his wooden dish. When we came back, all the nuggets were gone.

Closing the door and repairing any holes in the plywood walls of the enclosure did not help, as Mr. Chipmunk was still able to get in. Moreover, the sound of my power drill scared BK, who went into hiding underneath the ramp that went down into his pool. Perhaps BK was haunted by memories of the noisy excavator in St. Albans that had crushed his lodge with the rest of his family inside?

I failed to learn from this experience. Two days later I scared BK again when I tried to roust Mr. Chipmunk out of the enclosure by banging on the pool with a stick. Even though BK was in the Auld Cove with Laura, he heard the noise and hid under the cove's tree-root bank.

When BK did not come out for a while, Laura became afraid BK drowned. I knew beavers could hold their breath underwater for at least fifteen minutes, so I was confident BK was simply hiding. Sure enough, when I called for him, BK did come out, doing a fast swim around the Auld Cove before going right back under the bank. Evidently, BK wanted to check in with me to make sure *I* was OK before retreating to safety. It would be two hours before BK came out again and Laura and I could bring him back to the enclosure.

Eventually I hit upon a solution. I put nuggets in BK's dish only when he was present to eat them and placed the nugget dish inside the Dogloo, where BK could defend them from Mr. Chipmunk. The last time I saw Mr. Chipmunk was down by the stream when I was sitting on the bank watching BK swim around the Auld Cove. Mr. Chipmunk came running across a log stretching over the cove, then onto the bank, being so bold as to run underneath my chair and investigate my foot! Clearly Mr. Chipmunk was hungry for nuggets now that he was denied access to them in the enclosure. I gave one to him as a peace offering.

One day, when I arrived at the stream after Laura had walked BK down earlier and was sitting on the bank watching, I found him frantically busy, building a dam just upstream from the Auld Cove. A tree had come down on the downstream side of the Swimway and mud had piled up, blocking the stream, but BK was adding to it, piling sticks and pushing mud and wet leaves with his snout onto them, where they sank into the crevices. So this was how beavers built their dams! It was fascinating to watch. BK was so successful that water now was diverted to the left, running into the tree roots under which BK liked to hide. It quickly became obvious that beavers don't use their tails to build dams, as I remembered from way back when I used to watch Bugs Bunny cartoons as a kid. BK used his tail as a rudder/keel during swimming and to slap the water when scared, but he pushed mud around using his snout and his paws. When Laura attempted to bring BK back, he managed to escape from the enclosure, as we were busy filling his pool, and went down to the stream again. He was floating in the Auld Cove when I came down, and Laura had to entice him with his Beaver Buddy and carry him back. The siren call of the stream was strong!

For the rest of the month, BK continued with his dam building, developing skills he would need when he was out in the wild for good. He definitely made his Swimway deeper; he could now do dips and dives while swimming laps. One day, after moving around a lot of mud for his dam, BK encountered a flock of turkeys as he was waddling across our lawn with Laura to keep him company. The turkeys, who had come onto the lawn to eat grasshoppers, were just as startled as BK, flying into the trees to get away from the mad rampaging beaver! BK, on the other hand, wanted to run away from the mad rampaging turkeys, and Laura had to hold onto him tightly to keep him from rushing back into the stream.

BK had a close encounter with another animal on our lawn that month: Bugs (short for Lovebug), our cat. Laura had brought BK onto the lawn to dry out after swimming laps in his Swimway, and he was following her, waddling and galumphing across the grass. I opened the screen door to change his water in the enclosure, and Bugs came running across the lawn to meet BK! Perhaps the cat was curious about this creature that had kept her out of the bathroom (where she usually had her food dish) all those months. Laura stood in front of BK and put out her hands to stop Bugs, but she really wanted to meet the beaver. I got there just in time to persuade Bugs to turn around and go back into the house, after which I proceeded to change BK's water. But Bugs was dejected the whole rest of the day.

We spent time with BK in the enclosure, too. Aside from changing his water, we occasionally cleaned out the detritus that built up around his Dogloo, which included not only stick shavings but the stuffing from his dog bed, which he had ripped open. BK chewed and dug everything he could find, digging in the dirt down to the wire mesh that ran underneath the enclosure or chewing any wooden slats or supports not protected by mesh that he could pull

down. It was a constant battle to keep ahead of his incisors. Sometimes BK would not get out of his pool when
I wanted to change his water, or he would take down his
ramp, which I had to put back up again.

But there was still plenty of BK Time filled with tender,
loving moments when we were just there for cuddles and
companionship. For example, one morning Laura groomed
BK as he lay in her lap, and he groomed her back, using
his teeth on Laura's thick woolen sweater from Ireland,
which protected her skin. He sometimes rolled around
onto his back like a big roly-poly toy, showing us his belly
as he begged for nuggets, which was terribly cute.

As the weather turned colder during the month of
October, we tried putting some old hay and straw into
BK's Dogloo for insulation. But BK didn't seem to like the
straw, and we put in dry towels instead, which we had to
change often. Winter was coming and we'd have to find
a way to keep BK alive through its long, bitter months.

We didn't take BK out to the stream as much. It was
rainy for much of October, then it snowed, covering the
ground in white. The water in the stream became much
colder, making it much more unpleasant to fish BK out of
the water and carry him back to his enclosure. In the first
part of the month, leaves falling from the trees covered
the surface of the water, making for beautiful fall pictures
of BK with foliage on his back or his face as he swam. But
in the latter part of the month, the snow made footing

treacherous by the stream, and we could no longer safely carry BK there and back.

What were we to do with BK in the winter? We couldn't keep him warm enough in the Dogloo, even with lots of hay or straw for insulation. It was time, once again, to call Beaver Lady. She told me that if I could manage it, I should keep BK indoors all winter, especially in his first year. Young beavers simply do not have enough fat on their bodies to survive exposure to the cold, even with siblings or mates for company. Only with a family unit living all together, sharing their bodily warmth, was the temperature in the lodge a cozy seventy degrees Fahrenheit, as measured by biologists, studying beavers, who inserted a probe into the lodge in winter to measure its temperature. Without their family, orphaned beavers died of pneumonia in the lodge. Beaver Lady told me this had actually happened to rehabbers who left their beavers out for the winter, only to find them dead in the lodge by spring.

Left unsaid was this meant many young beavers—possibly in the hundreds or thousands—died every year in Vermont, orphaned when their parents or older siblings were trapped and they were left on their own to fend for themselves through the long winter months. For most animals, trapping seasons by design avoided such tragedies by starting in the late fall, by which time the young had fully matured and left their parents to strike out on their own. But young beavers didn't leave the colony until they were two—which meant no trapping season could avoid orphaning beavers. This is why trapping of beavers is so cruel.

As for BK, Laura and I decided we would keep him in our basement, which has a concrete floor and a drain for gray water that we could use to drain his water tank every day using a sump pump. At the moment, however, the basement was occupied by Oreo, a Dutch rabbit with black on his front and hind ends and white in the middle. He was owned by Laura's niece, Paige, and we were babysitting him until the end of the month. I joked with Paige about having beaver/bunny cage matches and taking bets from the local community as a way to finance my wildlife rehab. She didn't appreciate my sense of humor. But I'd bet BK would win.

BK had to survive in his outdoor enclosure until November. We put a heat lamp inside the enclosure, hanging just over the entrance to his Dogloo, at the end of October, when the evening temperature dipped to nineteen degrees Fahrenheit. The heat lamp kept BK nice and cozy in the dark. When we came in during night check to see how he was doing, he was swimming in his pool, the water still warm from the hot water tank. We also put plastic sheeting over the top and eastern sides of the enclosure, which were open to the elements, to help insulate BK from the blowing, biting wind.

During the last ten days of October, Laura started taking BK out during the day and letting him run around on the wraparound screened-in porch of our house. Normally this was the domain of Bugs, our cat, but Laura made sure she was locked inside. The first day BK was on our porch, I was standing just outside, changing BK's water in the pool of his enclosure. BK pressed his nose and his paws against the screen facing the enclosure, making a funny face like some people do when pressing against the glass of a car window. If Laura hadn't distracted him, BK may have chewed right through the screen to get to his dad standing on the other side! Even with winter coming on, covering the lawn with snow and icing over the stream, BK was able to get his exercise in his own private "mall walk."

3

Beaver in the Basement

After we said goodbye to Oreo at the beginning of November, we began to beaver-proof our basement. We knew that whatever enclosure material we chose had to be metal to keep BK from chewing right through it. I was at my wit's end as to what to do when one day, Laura happened to notice some decorative metal railings for sale at the local hardware store. We bought everything they had, three railings that were six feet long by four feet high, and one that was four feet long by four feet high. I arranged them in a six-by-ten-foot square space underneath the stairwell, the underside of which I covered in twelve-gauge wire mesh. I also wrapped the bottom third of two upright two-by-fours that were supporting the basement ceiling. I then incorporated a metal dog crate into the enclosure

to serve as BK's house, laid down two new rubber horse
stall mats to serve as cushioning against the cold, hard
concrete floor, and finally set up a two-by-four-foot
hard plastic water tub with a drain spigot to serve as his
pool. I also brought down BK's ramp from his enclosure
and installed it in the new pool. The basement was ready
to receive BK!

Already we were midway through the month. Fortunately, the first part of November had been mild, in the
forties and even fifties Fahrenheit. We were able to take
BK down to the stream a few times, where he mostly
stayed in the Auld Cove, honing his damming skills. He'd
dive into the water, dredge up a stick, and put it on the
right side of the dam, where the water was flowing. Then
he'd dig up some mud and leaves and pile that onto the
stick; then he'd put on a rock; then another stick, and so
on. Even though it was fascinating to watch BK's dam-
building, it was freezing cold to pluck BK out of the water
and carry his wet wiggling self home to the enclosure. We
continued to add hay and straw to his Dogloo and turned
on the heat lamp, especially on cold nights.

The first night BK spent in the basement was stressful
for him. This was only natural, as it was completely new
surroundings. For most of the night he hid under the short
side of the ramp inside the water tub, just like he did when
I made drilling noises outside his enclosure as I repaired
the hole through which Mr. Chipmunk snuck in to get

nuggets. This time, he also splashed water everywhere with his tail whenever one of us came clumping down the stairs or the furnace ignited. By the next night, however, BK had gotten used to the strange noises and was willing to come out and spend time with us in his new playpen. He was especially cuddly in the morning, when he would just sit in my lap and eat nuggets and he was still poufy and dry. In the evening, Laura and I usually kept BK company while watching a show or the news on our computer. It was in BK's company that we watched Trump lose to Joe Biden on election night, and later the January 6th Insurrection and the Second Impeachment Trial of Trump. BK was more interested in playing tug-of-war with a stick or a towel or one of his chew toys, just like a dog would do. Except BK could win the war simply by biting the stick in half and then taking his half away to nibble on, chewing the bark off as if he were eating corn on the cob.

BK enjoyed his new tub, even though it was too small for him to swim around in. But he compensated for that by kicking his legs in place in the water while holding onto the side of the tub with his forepaws, as if he were exercising in a lap-less swimming pool. The main problem with the tub was that BK was chewing the plastic to bits, so we had to get a metal tub of similar dimensions. The other problem was that the drain plug did not work, so we had to get a sump pump and drain the water that way, which worked pretty well. BK enjoyed his dog-crate house,

which we covered with towels to make it dark inside, and
we put a big furry pad on the floor that was nice and soft.
BK would lie on the pad, flattening his body so that he
looked like a rug on a rug! But he also liked to sit on it just
after getting out of the tub and groom his belly, rubbing
and scratching it like a Buddha. One day he nearly got
out of the enclosure when he piled sticks at one end of his
water tub, just underneath the stairs, so he could stand on
this makeshift platform and get over the railing. We had to
not only move the tub away from the railing but also add
another layer of wire mesh just underneath the stairs, because
BK was able to nibble on the wood between the one-inch
spacing of the wire.

A great advantage of BK being in the basement was that
we could spend a lot of time with him, which would have
been difficult if he had been outside in a cold enclosure.
He was in our lodge, but we tried to make it his lodge, too.

Much of the time was spent playing Beaver Wrestle,
with us grabbing whatever was to hand for BK to safely
push against without scratching us with his forepaws. BK
never used his teeth when he was wrestling; he was mainly
trying to push us over using his upper body strength and
his legs. BK was getting stronger and stronger, and going
through any number of stuffed animal proxies.

First, there was Catamount Puppet. This was an effective wrestling opponent, as it had two paw arms into which
I could insert my fingers and thus push more effectively

with my hand against BK. One day BK carried off Cata-mount Puppet after a bout of Beaver Wrestle. When we found the puppet later that day, it was ripped to shreds, its stuffing coming out of a great gash on the top of its head. I just felt lucky that it was the puppet that took the brunt of BK's frustrations with his wrestling buddy, not my hand!

Next, it was the turn of Big Teddy Bear. Big Teddy Bear had a size advantage, and we could use its bulk against BK, although he was now almost as big as Big Teddy Bear. BK was able to push both Laura and Big Teddy Bear across the concrete floor, which she could stop only by anchoring her back against a post or something else immovable. One day we found that BK had also murdered Big Teddy Bear. He had chewed a hole on the side of his face and on his nose, after which he began pulling all the stuffing out. Now Big Teddy Bear was not so big.

We were starting to run out of stuffed animal toys to play with. We had to resort to Mr. Lynx, which was the smallest of the toys thus far. BK hissed at Mr. Lynx at first because he was not familiar with it, but eventually he began wrestling with it. We also often used Wet Towel, which had more heft than a dry one, in order to play Beaver Wrestle. Then one day Laura came down to find BK shaking his hips in a funny way over Wet Towel. This made us think that perhaps he was starting to explore his sexuality and the towel was the lucky recipient of his atten-tions, although BK was still far too young to reach sexual maturity. Towel also had the advantage of being able to absorb BK's pee and castoreum, which he occasionally deposited on the floor of the enclosure.

Laura and I often tag-teamed our wrestling matches with BK, with one of us wrestling him from the front while the other cradled him from behind, ready to catch him if he fell over backward from having been bested in a match. When BK was tired from wrestling, he would lie on the floor and flatten his body like a rug. This was his relaxed, downtime mode but in no way a signal of submission. Pretty quickly, he would get up and challenge us to another wrestle.

Otherwise, we spent a lot of time grooming BK. He would come waddling over to us and simply "melt" his body into our laps. He was certainly a lapful: At the end of September, we weighed him in at twenty pounds, and early in the new year, he weighed in at thirty-three pounds! Because BK had so much fat, he could let his body relax and it would pour into whatever gap was available on our own bodies. While BK molded his flabby body into the space between our legs, he'd rest his head somewhere he could bury his face in, such as the crook of my arm or my crotch. BK often flattened himself on us while we were watching a show or some other program on my laptop. We then would comb his fur with the flea comb or scratch him with our hands. BK would groom us back, using his teeth on our skin but being very gentle, giving us love nibbles but never biting or breaking the skin. This must be how beavers in the wild spend cold winter days in the lodge, grooming each other or wrestling, although there would be far less room for that than in our basement!

These grooming sessions made me appreciate how integral BK's fur was to the rest of his body. The fur only really worked if BK was wearing it: He groomed it constantly, keeping it clean and well-oiled, and it dried fast after he came out of the water, no doubt due to BK's body heat warming it from the inside out. Once you separated the fur from the beaver's body, as trappers did, it became dry and crunchy, was much harder to clean, and took a very long time to dry if it got wet. I know this from my experience of cutting up fur coats to use as bedding for patients. To my skin, the furs felt scratchy and irritating; there was a reason why hair shirts—basically fur coats worn inside-out with the fur next to the body—were a form of penance and punishment in the Catholic Church. For many in the West, fur coats and hats were status symbols and little else, having little practical value as articles of clothing; however, Indigenous peoples placed different values on fur and had more sustainable relationships with furbearing animals than did the commercial fur trade.

In mid-December, BK's swimming situation got an update when Laura found a used metal stock tank for sale online—eight feet long by three feet wide by two feet high—at a former horse farm in Bethel. Since he had

moved into the basement, BK only had the small metal
tank where he could drink and poo, but do little else,
which had to be changed four times a day. Laura and I
were able to slide the new tank down the stairs and then
turn the corner into the basement, although we had to take
out both of the stair railings to do so. We set up the tank
along the basement's north wall and put in a Beavertail
ramp, made for dogs to get on boats easily, that Laura had
ordered by mail, which fit inside the tank perfectly, span-
ning its three-foot width exactly. (I found it most appro-
priate that a ramp named after beavers was actually being
used by one!) It had a steep upper part where it hung over
the side and then flattened out and dipped a little lower
so the bottom part formed a platform in the water. We put
a car mat rug over the topmost steep part to help BK gain
some traction. I built a wooden ramp to get into the tub,
screwing thin plywood onto the sides to serve as railings.
Finally, we put a length of four-by-four wood underneath
the east end of the tank, where the boat ramp was, so it had
a slight tilt, which would allow us to drain the tank more
easily at the opposite end. Filling the tank took a long time
given its three-hundred-gallon capacity. Laura also got
some more stall mats and metal railings, so we were able to
expand the enclosure area to include the large water tank,
effectively doubling the enclosure to the point that it took
up most of the basement itself! We still kept the original
footprint of BK's enclosure, effectively dividing the new,

larger enclosure in two in case we found a potential mate for BK and we could introduce them slowly, each in their own space.

We then let BK out from his side of the enclosure to explore his new large tank and play area. At first he didn't want to stray farther than the gate between the two sides. We almost had to carry him to the ramp, which he went up, but he was hesitant about going down the steep part into the tank on the other side. Eventually, we coaxed him down and he went into the water. He now had room to dip and dive, somersault and roll, all of which he did at the deeper west end. Initially he was wary of swimming underneath the boat ramp, but eventually he did and explored the small space at the east end as well. He then climbed back onto the ramp and launched himself back into the water, like a kid jumping into a swimming pool!

We had a hard time persuading him to get out of the tank. Things were not made any better when, approaching the tank, I surprised BK, and he slapped the water with his tail. This made a huge splash that dunked the whole of my face and upper half of my body, as if a car had sped through a big puddle and splashed me. Eventually we got BK out of the water and back into his smaller enclosure. The next day, it was Laura's turn to get splashed as she tried to fish BK out of the tank. We were able to do this only by working together to corral him at the shallow east end, where Laura was able to pick him up, all slippery, put

him on the ramp, towel him off, and then carry him back
to his side of the enclosure.

Soon BK became potty-trained. He went to the bathroom in his small, warmer pool, with Laura frequently
catching his poo in her hands as it came out so the water
wouldn't get too dirty. He then would get out, go through
the gate into the adjoining area with the large water tank,
go up the ramp, and have a swim in his larger pool. If he
had to go to the bathroom again, he would get out of
his large tank, go down the ramp, through the gate into his
own side of the enclosure with the small tank, go potty,
then go back across to his larger tank to swim some more.
We found his poo changed during the day. In the morning,
it was more solid, in the form of small pellets, but by
noon it was looser and larger. At the end of the day, it had
reverted to small, solid pellets. Perhaps he ate more woody
food at the crepuscular times of dawn and dusk, and then
Rodent Chow nuggets in between.

One day BK decided to be lazy and stayed in his dog-
crate house for the whole morning, lying in bed. When he
decided to come out, we let him into the large play area
beside the large water tank, where he just wanted to play
Beaver Wrestle on the stall mats with Laura and me. This
threatened to become BK's new routine. When he finally
grew tired of wrestling, he'd go into the large tank for a
swim. One day, after we left him swimming and came
back, we found that he had gone back into his own side of

the enclosure and even closed the gate behind him! Now, if he had locked it as well—by wrapping the chain around two railings that secured them together—I'd be seriously worried that he'd be ready to take over our farm, much like the pigs in Orwell's novel!

BK came to love his large water tank even more than playing Beaver Wrestle. Soon he was foregoing the latter and going straight into the tank. As soon as we opened the divider gate, he'd rush out like a racehorse, bound to the tank, and get in. We'd play with him in the water, getting him to do rolls in both directions (tickling his belly as he did so); 360-degree wheelies; and somersaults, which Laura called "whoop-de-dos," where he'd go end over end in the water like an otter. Laura and I also learned how to help BK swim in place in the large tank. We'd hold our arm or hand in the water and let him grab onto it with his paws like an overboard sailor clinging to a lifebuoy. He would then swim against us, much like he pushed against us on land when playing Beaver Wrestle. Laura said she could feel BK's heart rate go up as he did this, and I'm sure it was good aerobic exercise, helping to increase his stamina and strength.

The downside was that we now had to change the water in the large tank more often—every other day or so—which was a much longer chore than changing the smaller tank. It took about an hour, the first half of which involved draining the water with a sump pump, with the drain hose inserted into the basement floor drain by the stairs; the second half involved filling the tank with a hose connected to the hot water heater. One day, we came down to find that BK had chewed the new hose attached to the sump pump to bits. Somehow he had grabbed it through the bars and chewed off four small pieces and two longer ones. His work was impressive: The cut ends looked like they had been cut diagonally and cleanly with a knife or sharp razor.

For Christmas, we gave BK two Jolly Balls, one red, one green, for him to play with. These were toys that we normally gave to our horses out in the pasture, but we found they also floated in water, and BK would push them around the tank with his nose. He also grabbed them by the handle with his teeth and carried them out of the tank and all the way back to his house. We also gave him some cardboard for Christmas, which he loved to chew. We found this out when one day BK got out of his pen because some of the railings were not securely zip-tied together, and he chewed one of the cardboard boxes that stored our stuff. Fortunately, he was only interested in chewing cardboard, not what was contained therein.

As we closed out the year, BK was becoming a night owl, staying up later in the evening and then lying in bed for longer in the morning. If we tried to rouse him, he'd become cranky and hiss at us. When he finally got up, he wanted to play either Swimming-in-Place in the large tank or Beaver Wrestle on the rubber stall mats. As we rang in the New Year, watching the ball drop on our computer, BK stayed up with us past midnight, swimming in his tank.

Even though Oreo was gone, BK was far from alone in the basement at this time. The first to keep him company was a snowy owl, who arrived at the end of the first week in December. She came from Irasburg in the Northeast Kingdom, comprising the northeast corner of Vermont, where she was probably part of an irruption of juveniles, born in a good breeding year, that had migrated farther south than their normal habitat on the Arctic tundra. I knew right away that she was a female because of her distinctive plumage: abundant dark horizontal barring on her chest and wings on a snowy white background; males typically are almost pure white in plumage. She was thin and starving, with a sharp keel and weighing in at only 1722 grams. (Female snowy owls typically weigh over two kilograms.) A farmer discovered her in his cow barn, where she had wandered in perhaps looking for food; the tips of her wing feathers were covered in cow manure. Nonetheless, she was still a magnificent creature, with her big yellow eyes, huge furry talons, and wingspan of four to five feet.

With starving patients like this, we have an Emaciation Protocol. For the first twenty-four hours, one cannot give them any food, which would actually kill them because their emaciated, dehydrated bodies simply can't handle it. Instead, I bypass the GI tract altogether and rehydrate them by injecting fluids—such as a lactated ringer's solution—underneath the skin, which I typically do on their back on either side of the spine. As I'm injecting, a bubble of water forms just under the distended skin, which will be directly absorbed into the body. This is really no different than a drip feed at the hospital.

After three such doses of subQ (subcutaneous) fluids, administered twelve hours apart, one can proceed to some oral feeding, on the assumption that the patient is sufficiently hydrated. We then gradually introduce some sort of easily digestible protein to build the patient toward solid food.

The snowy owl received 60 cc of Normasol with each subQ dose, making for a total of 180 cc, or three-quarters of a cup, injected into her back under the skin. She responded well to this treatment, perching and growing more feisty each time I took her out of the Intensive Care Ward, a two-by-two-foot square by three-foot high wooden box that allowed the bird free movement, but not so much that she overexerted herself.

It was now the second day, and the owl was sufficiently hydrated; I could tell because the skin on her back was less dry and more pinkish. It was time to introduce some oral nutrition. I used Emeraid, a protein powder that you mix with water, which I tubed 50 cc at a time. Tubing involves putting a rubber tube down the right side of the owl's throat in order to deliver food directly to the stomach, without the owl having to swallow or risk getting food aspirated into the airway. Unfortunately, owls have no crop or pouch in the esophagus, which makes tubing easy in other birds. Nonetheless, the snowy owl took this fine, but I noticed that her poo looked black and yellow, which was an ominous sign. By the fourth day, I had switched her to an A/D slurry, consisting of a prescription wet dog food cut with water, slightly more nutritious than Emeraid. I continued with A/D for three more days, but by the seventh day, the owl was vomiting all her A/D and her poo was pure A/D, having not been digested at all. So I switched her back to Emeraid, which the owl tolerated well. In the meantime, I had a fecal analysis done, and it was found that no less than three different types of parasites were in her gut, including roundworm! That meant that I had to worm her, which I did with Ivermectin, while at the same time I continued to tube the owl on Emeraid for five more days. Her poo started looking normal—dark brown spots in a white urea—a good sign for recovery.

I next started the snowy owl on her first solid food: raw chicken breast. Chicken breast is pure meat, with no skin, bone, or fur for the owl to cough up as a pellet. At first I had to pop chicken pieces directly into her mouth, but soon she began to eat it right out of my fingers, tearing the meat greedily and swallowing it on her own. This was an encouraging sign. The next evening she ate ten mice out of my hand, and the next day, on Christmas Eve, I decided to put her outside, in the aviary, for the first time. She had been cooped up in the Intensive Care Ward for two and a half weeks now, so I felt it was time she got some fresh air. But by the next day—Christmas—it was clear that she was too weak to fly. I found her on the ground, soaked from the rain that fell in the night. At least the rain had washed away the cow manure on her feathers and she was now all clean. Since it was supposed to get cold that evening, I brought her back inside.

Although she had started eating on her own, it was clear the snowy owl was still losing weight and, in fact, she was dying. During the last week of the owl's life, I tried everything to save her. I gave her Emeraid, chicken breast, and cut-up mice, all of which she managed to keep down, but her weight remained stubbornly well below what it had been when she had first come in. I was baffled. It was as if she was unable to absorb into her body what she was eating. My vet and a fellow raptor rehabber both thought all the parasites in her gut may have compromised her ability to digest food. During the last two days of her life, I put the owl back out in the aviary to give her a last taste of freedom and the wild. On the second day of the New Year, I brought her back inside and gave her some more wormer and Emeraid. I weighed her and she was now at 1450 grams, nearly 300 grams below her incoming weight. When I checked on her a couple hours later, she was dead. I mourned the loss of such a magnificent and beautiful creature.

I had better success, however, with two other, more common, animals that I also took in that December. One was a mink, which came to me about a week after I got the snowy owl. He was hit on the left side of his face by a car in Barre, causing it to swell, including around his eye, which was swollen shut. The vet examined him and said his jaw wasn't broken but everything was realigned, or dislocated, to the right, so the mink's left upper incisor was now on the inside of his lower canine, instead of the other way around. Since the mink could still chew and use his jaw, he had a chance of being fully rehabbed and released back into the wild. However, I had to wear PPE—latex gloves and a mask—whenever handling him, per Vermont Department of Fish and Wildlife guidelines, since mink were highly susceptible to coronavirus. In fact, Denmark had culled seventeen million farm-raised mink—its entire domestic mink population—the previous month, in November, owing to outbreaks of COVID-19 at several farms, where it was feared the virus would mutate and spread in an even more virulent form from mink to humans. However, outbreaks were much more rare among wild mink, owing to far less contact between humans and animals. The PPE was as much to protect the wild mink population as it was to protect humans.

For all of that first day and the next two, the mink simply slept on his towel in the carrier. Maybe this was because he had been given some drugs for the pain and inflammation, but he also clearly needed some rest and recovery time. I put in some A/D and a small dish of water, which he didn't touch for the first day. By the second day, however, I noticed some teeth marks and a chunk missing from the A/D, and on the third day he had drunk from and/or knocked over his water dish, which was lying on its side. He was now looking up at me from his bed whenever I changed his food or water dish. On the fourth day, he was up and about in his carrier, looking at me through the bars, and I knew we had to change his circumstances and give him a bigger space.

Laura and I carried the large cage that I used to rehab weasels down into the basement. The cage consisted of a linoleum-covered plywood floor and four walls and a hinged roof made out of coated half-inch wire stapled onto wood frames. I also put in a wooden nest box with some bedding cut from a mink coat, an exercise wheel, some wood shavings spread around the floor, his food dish, and a round rubber horse feed tub that would serve as his larger water dish. We then took the carrier, put it in the cage, opened the door, and tipped it. At first, the mink didn't want to come out and clung to the sides of the carrier. But we tipped it nearly vertical, and he fell out and began exploring his new environment. He lapped at the water and even jumped in it, sniffed at his food dish (which contained

A/D and a mouse cut in two), put half of his body in the exercise wheel, then squeezed into the nest box. He seemed to be happy in his new home.

Over the next nine days, before Christmas, I was able to observe the mink in his cage. On the first day, I didn't see him all day, as he seemed to be sleeping in his nest box. But I knew that he came out at night as a big chunk of A/D was missing and the shavings were wet by the water tub. The next day the mink came out of his nest box in the daytime, and I watched him eat all his A/D. He also took sips of his water, which I had just changed, and tasted the mouse I had cut in half for him but didn't eat any of it. He also jumped on top of his nest box and then jumped down and rubbed himself in the shavings and lay down briefly in them. At one point he looked directly at me with his beady eyes. On day three I saw him eat a mouse I had cut into small pieces, so I knew he could use his jaw to chew and I didn't have to feed him A/D anymore.

On the fourth day, I came downstairs in the morning and the mink was already up and about, climbing all over his cage, even hanging from the roof by his claws! He was clearly impatient for his food. I didn't know how I would be able to open the top in order to drop in his mice, until, when I went to unlatch the top, the mink solved my problem by quickly slipping into his nest box to hide. I blocked the hole and put in three cut-up mice, about fifty grams, and then another three mice in the evening, for a total of one hundred grams or about 10 percent of his body weight. The next day I fed the mink a whole mouse cut in half, which I saw him eat just fine, tearing apart the mouse's flesh with his teeth. In the evening I blocked him in his nest box again in order to clean up some of his scat, which was both in the exercise wheel and in the shavings.

For the next two days, I kept feeding the mink whole mice while I tried to catch a live mouse in the small Havahart trap to conduct a live prey test. The mink was getting more active, to the point that I had to change the shavings because they got all wet from him splashing in his water tub and running around his cage. Finally, on the eighth day, I caught a wild mouse in the trap and put it in with the mink. At first the mouse hid behind the nest box, and the mink didn't even notice it when he came out. But eventually, he saw the mouse and went after it. The mouse was quick, but the mink was quicker. In a few seconds it was all over. The mouse lay dead at the mink's feet, but the mink didn't eat it right away; instead he cached it under some shavings. Later the mink looked desperate to get out of his cage, climbing the walls and the roof and baring his teeth. But when I took the snowy owl out to feed her, she looked at the mink as if she would fly right out of my hands and grab and eat him. The mink noticed this and promptly scooted back into the safety of his nest box. The hunter became the hunted!

Early in the morning on Christmas Eve, we decided to release the mink. I placed a piece of cardboard over the opening of the nest box and lifted it out of the cage and carried it outside. Laura wanted to release him across the river, so we waded through the freezing cold water. I set the box underneath the shelter of some trees and removed the cardboard. The mink stuck his head out and sniffed the air. After a while, he emerged and explored his surroundings. He scampered underneath some logs, then scurried across the stream back toward the outdoor enclosure! Then we lost sight of him. Later, I found his tracks by the side of the house and thought he might be living under our porch, despite all our efforts to keep him away from the house by carrying him across the stream! However, five days later I visited the nest box and found the mink was still using it. A scrap of mink coat had been pulled halfway out of the opening in order to block it up, and I could hear him sighing inside. I put in two whole mice and pieces of a third in the hole to tide him over and placed another scrap of mink coat fur-side down over the top of the box and over the hole to help him keep warm. Eventually the mink found another home, as there were no longer tracks around the nest box and the mice I had put inside were rotting, untouched. He was now living on his own.

I had one last adventure with a wild animal before the New Year. It began on the Winter Solstice, December 21, and also ended on Christmas Eve. Around 4:00 P.M. on the Solstice, just as it was getting dark, I got a panicked call from a woman out in a house in Fayston, about forty minutes

away west, over the mountain. She claimed that there was
something caught in a chimney flue that started making a
ruckus when she tried to start a fire in the grate. She said
it was her parents' place and that she was just looking in to
check on things and make sure everything was OK.

It was completely dark when I got to the house. I found
the woman sitting in her car, afraid to go back inside. I put
a mask on and she let me in, not daring to go in herself.
The first thing I did was to take off my shoes in order
not to track mud across the carpet of what looked like an
upscale ski chalet built in the seventies. I soon found the
fireplace, which was an open hearth, but the chimney had
a metal sleeve going all the way through it, with the flue set
way high up. I gingerly peered through the open flue and
saw a flash of an owl's feathers. I put on my supple leather
falconry gloves—which offered good protection but were
not so thick that I couldn't manipulate the fingers—and
reached up and managed to grab hold of a foot. I then
gently pulled down a little, got hold of the other foot,
and pulled until a whole owl emerged. I cradled him in
my arms. It was a small barred owl. He was thin, having
been trapped in there at least a day, but it couldn't have been
much more than that because there was still some flesh
on him. He was very feisty. I brought him outside in the
carrier and showed him to the woman sitting in her car.

"Well, at least it's not Santa caught in the chimney!" She
put some bills in my hand (a donation, as all rehabbers

work on a volunteer basis). When I counted it out later, it was one hundred bucks.

When I brought the owl home, he was still very feisty, hanging off the metal door grate and going from side to side in the carrier as I tried to weigh him. When I took him out to examine him, there seemed nothing wrong with his legs or wings; he was just a little thin. I gave him 20 cc of Emeraid and started him on A/D the next day, followed shortly thereafter with some raw chicken meat. By the third day, I was feeding him whole mice, of which he gobbled down at least half a dozen. This was an accelerated Emaciation Protocol, as the owl seemed to be hungry but not starving, nor sick like Snowy.

On the morning of Christmas Eve, after I had released the mink, I put the barred owl out in the aviary just to see if he could fly. He flew right up to one of the feeding platforms from the ground, confirming he was strong enough to get lift from his wings, and I knew he was ready to be released. As it was getting toward dusk, around 3:00 P.M., Laura and I took the barred owl back over to Fayston and set him on a bare patch of grass by the house where I had rescued him. It was a warm, mild day, the temperature in the forties, a good day for a release. He looked at us and then flew to the branch of a nearby tree, then hopped to higher branches and surveyed us from his safe perch. We left him there, master of his domain.

4

The Mating Game

*W*elcome to the Mating Game! A game where a bachelor beaver must choose a lifelong mate from among three comely Beaverettes! Remember, folks, this game is mandated by biology! Beavers are hardwired to form families! A singleton beaver released into the wild will not stay in any location, but will roam for miles in search of a mate. That's why we try to mate them before they're released! That way, they'll stay in the beautiful release site we find for them!

And now, let's meet our lucky bachelor beaver, BK!

BK is a nearly one-year-old male beaver who likes to wrestle, chew sticks, and take moonlight swims in his favorite water tank! BK is being raised by humans, but don't let that fool you. This guy has a wild, independent streak! He has a beautiful tail and striking reddish-brown fur! BK has been on his own *for eight months and is now ready to share his life with some lucky Beaverette!*

And now, let's meet our three Beaverettes!

Beaverette #1 is called Pumpkin. She's also being raised by a rehabber, down in southern Vermont, where her mother was run over by a car. She had two siblings but lost them to diarrhea and some kind of intestinal disorder. Pumpkin also had diarrhea but survived, though now she has a deformed tail! Pumpkin is feeling lonely and ready for some companionship! But, she's harboring a secret! How will BK react? We'll find out!

Beaverette #2 is a two-year-old wild child, raised by some beavers in Stowe. She dispersed from her colony, got mauled by a dog, and suffered some deep bite wounds in her rear end! She's in recovery and hobbles around, lookin' for some tender lovin'! But she's older and wiser than your average yearling, having learned some rad skills in the wild! Now, she can help any domestic beaver adjust to life on the outside!

Beaverette #3 is a bug-eyed beauty from Benson, an orphaned yearling like BK and Pumpkin. Raised by a rehabber in New Hampshire, who named her Jelly, she lost her mate, Bean, when they were left outside in the lodge during their first winter. Now she's ready for love again, and to share her lodge-building skills with someone special!

So, who will it be, BK? Beaverette #1? Beaverette #2? Or Beaverette #3? Time to decide!

As we turned the page on a new year, we started looking for a mate for BK. This was both for him and for us. BK needed a friend, a companion, a playmate. He needed someone else to play Beaver Wrestle with besides humans. He also needed someone to share his water tank and snuggle with when he bedded down for the night.

We needed a break from all the attention we'd been giving BK. My arms and back were starting to hurt from all the Beaver Wrestling. And we worried about BK once he was released. Would he be able to survive on his own in the wild? One day, as we were playing Beaver Wrestle with BK, Laura suddenly burst out crying. I asked her, what was the matter? She said she was just thinking about how BK might get caught in a trap if he was alone and wandering, looking for a mate. But if he was already mated, he'd just stay put in one place. A mate for BK would alleviate much of our worry.

I imagined this search for BK's mate as a variation on *The Dating Game*, which I watched on TV as a kid. Normally a bachelorette would interview three bachelors, but occasionally a bachelor would interview three bachelorettes. BK was the beaver bachelor, and I found him three beaverettes to choose from. In reality, it was mostly Laura and I who were doing the choosing on BK's behalf.

Our first contestant to appear in our "studio" in early January was a beaver by the name of Pumpkin. Pumpkin was the sole surviving beaver from a litter of three orphaned

kits taken in by a rehabber in southern Vermont. Prior to
Pumpkin's arrival, Laura and I had paid her a visit as part
of our vetting process. Pumpkin seemed sweet and low-
key, but her tail was deformed, as if it had been squeezed
on the sides and had its circulation cut off. The underside
of the tail had a pink streak down the middle where scales
should have been. Pumpkin's mom told us this was all
due to massive diarrhea she had when she was younger,
whereby her tail simply sat in excrement for days. It seemed
curious that her siblings also had diarrhea and apparently
died from it. We wondered if Pumpkin would be releas-
able back into the wild with the raw underside to her tail.
Would it be rubbed and become more raw and get infected,
with the tail dragging on the ground all the time?

If this was a mark against Pumpkin, it only got worse.
When Pumpkin arrived on the first Sunday of January,
she was drooling from the stress of a two-hour car ride.
We tried to introduce BK and Pumpkin on "neutral"
territory—the aviary where I usually rehabbed raptors. The
two beavers ignored each other and, as dark was coming
on, we moved them into their separate enclosures in the
basement. Pumpkin immediately went up the ramp into
the large tank, where she hid under the Beavertail ramp
with just her nose peeking out. It took Laura an hour and
a half to entice her out of the water, where Laura tried to
win Pumpkin over by grooming her. BK was only interested in playing Beaver Wrestle with me, except for a few

moments when he peeked at Pumpkin through the bars
of the railing.

The next day, Pumpkin's mom came to visit and Pumpkin immediately came over to her, chittering and happy.
When I came downstairs after doing horse chores, I found
both Laura and Pumpkin's mom, wearing masks, cradling
their respective beavers in their laps on either side of the
railing dividing the two enclosures. Later, Pumpkin's mom
played with Pumpkin in the large tank, having Pumpkin
do rolls in the water and then swimming away and back
to her. After Pumpkin's mom left, we weighed Pumpkin
at twenty-three pounds, about ten pounds lighter than
BK. When we tried to play with Pumpkin in the large
tank, she slapped her tail at us and drenched us both with
water. Evidently, it was going to take a while for her to
accept us, and BK.

For the next two weeks, we tried to win Pumpkin over
while, at the same time, not neglecting BK. The morning
after her mom left, I found Pumpkin sitting on the ground
by the large tank, facing the wall and drooling. When I
tried to pet her, she hissed at me. The next day, Pumpkin
was chewing on the sides of the wooden ramp going into
the large tank, which we considered an improvement over
hiding away from us under the Beavertail ramp inside the
tank. By the fourth day, Pumpkin was imitating BK and
using the small pool—the plastic one that we had used
early on but had taken out because BK was chewing on

it—as her litterbox, leaving the large tank for swimming. She seemed to have learned this from watching BK while standing and holding onto the bars as BK swam just on the other side of her in his own small tank, the metal one.

We continued to try to win Pumpkin over, but she still hissed at me and BK, although Laura was able to get her to chitter and relax and flatten her body by scratching her backside incessantly—if she stopped, then Pumpkin began hissing again. Pumpkin could also be somewhat appeased with apples. We then tried swapping the beavers—putting BK in Pumpkin's enclosure and Pumpkin in BK's, to see if they could get used to each other's scents. BK went straight into the large tank, where he had fun doing rolls in the water, swimming against my hand, and floating on his back and letting me tickle his tummy. But we did see the two beavers touch noses through the railing divider for the first time, and they didn't hiss at each other, which we took as a good sign.

The next day, we came down to find BK—who was still in Pumpkin's side of the enclosure—had moved or swapped out all of his bedding. His fur-lined pad and towels, which Laura had moved into Pumpkin's side of the enclosure, right next to the railing divider, had been moved as far away from Pumpkin as possible. It was at the other end of the enclosure. Then BK had moved Pumpkin's dog-crate pad—which I recognized from the horse-themed decorations—over to where Pumpkin now was, on his side of the enclosure, evidently by pushing it through the bars of the railing. It was as if he was saying to Pumpkin: "This is mine and that is yours." We also found BK's fur-lined pad now had a reddish-brown, musky-smelling, oily stain—castoreum; evidently, BK had secreted this onto his pad the night before.

On the third Monday of January—Martin Luther King Jr. Day—everything came to a head. After two weeks of the beavers getting to know each other on either side of the railing, we decided to open everything up and introduce them directly to each other, with us in the enclosure as chaperones. We let Pumpkin out of the small enclosure, and she came ambling into the larger one, where BK was by the large tank. She wandered about for a bit and then came face to face with BK. Suddenly, they were attacking each other, biting and scratching with vicious abandon! Laura got in between them with the Big Teddy Bear and tried to separate them. But she was in her bare feet, and I warned her to get out of there. The beavers went at each other again, and BK bit Laura on the ankle as he was lunging at Pumpkin. I hurriedly shepherded BK back into the small enclosure, while Laura screamed in pain and ran upstairs, leaving a trail of bright red spots along the way. She sat in the bathtub, bleeding. There were two deep bite marks, one on each side of her left ankle. They were curved, matching the curves of BK's incisors.

We poured hydrogen peroxide on the wounds, but the deeper one started to swell. We bandaged the ankle with an ice pack, and I took Laura to the emergency room. They flushed Laura's wounds and put her on antibiotics, but they did not stitch up the wounds, preferring to let them drain. They said Laura was lucky—the bites had come within a "hair's breadth" of cutting the Achilles tendon, which would have meant that Laura couldn't walk again. When they asked how the bite happened, we told them that Laura had gotten in the middle of a fight between two of our pet "rodents."

The next day, I called Beaver Lady. After describing the disastrous courtship between BK and Pumpkin, the first words out of Beaver Lady's mouth were, "You have two beavers of the same sex." She said that the only time she had ever observed aggressive behavior in beavers was when two of the same sex were vying for the same territory. That would explain why BK was depositing all that castoreum, and why he switched all that bedding. I knew BK was a male: His os penis had showed up on the x-ray. That would mean Pumpkin was no longer a she, but a he! Pumpkin's mom had assured me Pumpkin had been x-rayed and no os penis had shown up on the film. But this must've been a false negative because they took the x-ray wrong. Beaver Lady said if Pumpkin really had been a female, BK would've taken to her almost right away, because a beaver's instinct is to form family units.

The next day, I called Pumpkin's mom to give her the news. She was shocked that Pumpkin was a male, but agreed her vet may have taken the x-ray from the back and not from the belly. She was more than happy to come and take Pumpkin back, as she had been missing him terribly. I asked her if she would change his name now that she knew he was a male. "Oh no. She'll always be Pumpkin to me."

On the last Monday of the month, a week from when Laura got bitten, Pumpkin's mom came up to take away Pumpkin. There was a palpable sense of relief on both sides. Our horse vet came to take another x-ray, this time of Pumpkin. Pumpkin's mom put on the lead apron and held Pumpkin in her lap with his back against her so the vet could take a couple of x-rays of the beaver's lower abdomen. The x-rays clearly showed the os penis. It was official. Pumpkin was a male.

After Mr. Pumpkin left with his mom, we rearranged the railings downstairs and made BK's enclosure bigger and more open. As he explored the other side of the enclosure where Pumpkin had been, BK hissed, particularly in a spot by the large tank where Pumpkin had deposited some castoreum. I cleaned this up, including underneath the stall mat, until when BK went back he didn't hiss at all. For good measure, BK deposited his own castoreum on his fur-lined pad and moved that over the spot where Pumpkin's castoreum had been. Just before bed, Laura came back upstairs and reported that BK had been swimming around in the large tank and had then got out and galumphed around his big new enclosure! He was alone and had us all to himself again and couldn't have been happier!

For the next two months, February and March, we spoiled BK with all the love and attention he could wish for. He'd sleep the morning away, until at least eleven o'clock, and then crawl into our laps for some grooming, play Beaver Wrestle, or else play with us in the large tank, especially Swimming-in-Place using our hand or arm, which he would grab and hold against his chest. It was during the grooming sessions that we felt two small lumps, one on BK's right flank, the other by the base of his tail. These must have been where Pumpkin had bitten him, not hard enough to break the skin, but enough to cause a swelling. Perhaps BK thought it was Laura who bit him, and that's why he bit her back; that was Laura's explanation. I believe Laura simply got in the way as BK lunged to strike back at Mr. Pumpkin.

By this time, Laura was comfortable enough to be in her bare feet around BK again, although she got a little nervous if he started sniffing her toes. As for me, I'd often greet BK with my own special greeting—which was to stick my finger in his mouth. Partly, this was a trust exercise: I knew that if he wanted to, BK could simply bite down on my finger and chomp it clean off, like I'd seen him do countless times to a stick he was chewing on. But BK never did; he was always very gentle, scraping my skin ever so slightly with the edge of his incisors. I must confess I always got a thrill from feeling BK's teeth on my skin: a short adrenaline shot of danger, all the while knowing you were safe from harm. Eventually, this greeting became a symbol of our unique bond—the fact that no other human could reasonably expect to shove a finger in a beaver's mouth and still withdraw it intact.

By mid-February, Laura had figured out a new way to play Beaver Wrestle that was less stressful on our arms. Instead of pushing against BK, which pitted the whole force of the beaver's body against the strength of our arm(s), Laura rolled up a towel and wrapped the middle of it around his mouth and then let him pull as she held on to both ends of the towel. It was as if she was riding a small, furry horse, with the towel in his mouth as a kind of bit. This way, BK was pulling against himself and his own weight, and he was far less likely to fall over and hurt himself or to hurt us. But I never got the hang of beaver riding!

It was also in February that we got foolproof confirmation that BK was a male. After the experience with Pumpkin, we now had a sliver of our own doubts. But one day, when BK was sitting on his tail and grooming himself, Laura saw his penis suddenly poke itself out from his cloaca! She said that it looked like a long red feeding nipple.

In March, Laura figured out a new way to play BK's other favorite game: Swimming-in-Place. In this variation,

Laura would push BK back in the water, then let him swim forward, then push him back again, and so on. We also found an easy way to get him to do 360-degree wheelies, which was to hold on to one end of Beaver Toy, while BK held on to the other end with his mouth, and then we pulled Beaver Toy and BK around in circles. I could also do this same exercise simply by getting BK to grab onto my finger or hand with his paws and pulling him around that way. All this was interspersed with somersaults, rolls, and belly rubs as BK floated on his back.

BK continued to be an escape artist. He escaped at least twice by chewing through the zip ties holding the bottom part of two railing panels together, thereby being able to slip through the gap even if the top part still held. The first time, Laura found him by the Intensive Care Ward I used for birds. The second time, he was at the other end of the basement, behind the oil furnace and the stacked totes we used to store stuff. In neither case did he chew anything or cause any damage; he just seemed to be sightseeing, exploring the furthest reaches of our basement.

In April, it was time for the next round of the Mating Game! We got a new contestant, Beaverette #2! And a third contestant was waiting in the wings, Beaverette #3!

First, we met Beaverette #2. A week before the end of April, I got a call from a husband and wife who lived on Main Street in Stowe. They had found a beaver in their backyard, all banged up and smelling terrible, which they had managed to corral into their garbage pail. We met at the Park-N-Ride in Montpelier, where I laid the garbage pail on its side on the ground, with the open gate of my carrier against it, and the beaver walked right into the carrier. It was a young beaver, small. At home I weighed her in at just fourteen pounds. This was less than half the weight of BK, who weighed in at thirty-eight pounds! Yet this beaver was probably twice BK's age, since kits disperse from their home territory when they are two years old. This was a testament either to the harsh living conditions in the wild or to the luxurious lifestyle we provided BK (or perhaps to both). The new beaver undoubtedly got into trouble when she traveled south from the Little River in Stowe in search of new territory; she then got attacked and bitten by something—most likely a dog—leaving two great puncture wounds on either side of her hindquarters.

When I got home, Laura helped me deposit the beaver into our bathtub, which we filled partway. The beaver immediately drank some water and did some poo. We then drained the tub and Laura held the beaver down with some towels over its face while I doused the wounds with Betadine solution and gave it a 1 cc shot of Baytril, an antibiotic. We then shepherded her back into the carrier and brought her to the outdoor enclosure, which still had the Dogloo and the plastic garden pool. We filled the pool with some warm water and let the beaver swim for a bit. When she clambered onto the ramp, the poor thing looked exhausted, as if she had been through hell and back.

The next morning, I checked in on Miss Beaver in the outdoor enclosure, half expecting to find her lying dead. But she was still alive! She had actually eaten something, judging by the absence of the apples and carrots and the chew marks on a large willow branch, all of which Laura had put in the previous night. Later, in the early afternoon, Laura and I went in and cleaned her wounds with more Betadine scrub. Some pus oozed out on one side where the wound was deep, but the wounds didn't smell anymore. I also gave her another shot of Baytril and put her in the pool, where she did some poo. We then put her back in the Dogloo with some apple and carrot pieces in front of her face. She immediately ate the food. Nonetheless, she was very thin, and she just lay on her towels all day.

On Monday, we took Miss Beaver to see the vet. After the vet put her to sleep in a plexiglass gas chamber, he used an electric clipper to shave some fur on the left hindquarters, where the biggest wound was. It turned out to be pretty ugly. There was a two-to-three-inch gash in the hide, with the bloody muscle showing underneath. The vet stitched up most of the wound, leaving a small hole for any pus or infection to drain out. He also cut off a lot of dead tissue, estimating that she had the wound for about a week. The wound on the right side was much smaller and not nearly so deep. Miss Beaver also had a superficial scrape on her belly and a shallow gash on the base of her tail. To combat any potential infection, the vet gave her a shot of Convenia, a long-term (i.e., lasting two weeks) antibiotic, and also a rabies shot. He then took a couple of x-rays, one from the side and one from the abdomen. Miss Beaver had no broken bones (thank goodness!) and no penis bone (she was a female!). After we put her back in the carrier, the vet instructed me to bathe the stitched wound once a day with Betadine solution and then some honey, which has natural healing powers. After we got home, Laura and I put Miss Beaver back in the outdoor enclosure, and Laura gave her some apples and carrots, which she ate greedily. Meanwhile, I visited BK and told him about his new potential girlfriend.

The remaining days of April were taken up with our daily routine of trying to heal all of Miss Beaver's wounds by flushing them with Betadine and then applying honey, as per the vet's instructions. Initially we did this in the enclosure, but eventually we resorted to putting her into the carrier and taking her into our bathroom, where we then treated her in the bathtub, half-filled with water, so at the same time she could drink her fill, poop, and have a little swim. They say that hydrotherapy is the best physical therapy because the flotation properties of water reduce the stress on recovering limbs and joints during exercise. There was the added benefit that warm water aided in the process of cleaning and flushing out her wounds of their pus and other gunk. We always followed the same order of treatment: First, we flushed the largest, stitched-up, wound on the left side, which had to be flushed several times using a special curved-tip irrigation syringe that we were able to insert just under the skin in the hole left unsewn by the vet. Miss Beaver barely tolerated this and made her displeasure known with hisses, grunts, and other noises of complaint. Then we flushed the smaller wound, on the right side, followed by the tiny fissures on her right hind foot and on her tail. Afterward, we put her back on a clean, dry towel in her Dogloo with some thick willow sticks, which she seemed to especially enjoy chewing, along with some apples and carrots. In addition, we introduced her to Mazuri Rodent Chow nuggets. By morning, they were all gone.

Laura and I were still trying to decide if Miss Beaver, or Beaverette #2, was the right mate for BK. She was definitely a female (confirmed by x-ray). She was probably two years old, so more mature than BK. That meant she had likely learned some "rad" skills in her time out in the wild, such as how to build a dam or build a lodge. But her age also could be a liability. Beavers sexually mature by age 3, but females mature earlier than males and can mature as early as 2.5 years. So it was entirely possible that Miss Beaver could become pregnant and then give birth to a litter of kits by this time next year, in the spring of 2022. That would make our release of the beavers much

more complicated. We'd also be accused by the Vermont
Department of Fish and Wildlife (VDFW) of running a
beaver breeding program!

Miss Beaver was recovering well from her wounds now
that we were treating them on a daily basis. She was eating
and pooping regularly, so her gut was in good working
order. But Miss Beaver was still very logy, just lying in
her Dogloo with her hindfeet flipped backward, looking
as if she was almost dead. We still had to carry her
into the pool, or into the bathtub, to make sure she got
access to water, and she always looked exhausted when
we put her back in her Dogloo. What if she never fully
recovered her mobility, and never could be released?
We wouldn't know the answer to this question for a
couple of months, so we continued her rehab. In the
meantime, we had an opportunity to interview a third
contestant, Beaverette #3. At the very least, I felt we
should meet her!

It was mid-April when this third beaver was brought to
my attention by a New Hampshire rehabber and veteri-
narian. Around this same time last year, a Vermont rehabber found an orphaned female beaver kit in Vermont
and offered it to the New Hampshire rehabber, who had
been looking for a mate for her male kit orphaned in New
Hampshire. (Truly, 2020 was the year of orphaned beaver
kits!) But now the New Hampshire rehabber wanted to
send the female kit—to whom she had given the name

of Jelly—back to her home state (i.e., to me). The reason was that Jelly's mate, Bean, had died over the winter from pneumonia. Even though the two had built a lodge in their outdoor enclosure, they simply did not have enough combined body mass to make the lodge warm enough to survive. Here was yet more proof of trapping's cruelties: How many young beavers—orphaned when their parents or older siblings were killed by trappers—endured long, cold deaths unseen in the lodge?

Jelly had a respiratory infection, but this was caught early enough that she was able to be treated with antibiotics and recover. I also needed to make sure Jelly was a female. The vet assured me she was, as she had x-rayed Jelly herself, and Jelly had gotten along with a confirmed male, Bean. That seemed good enough for me.

We agreed to do a hand off next month, in May, as that was when orphaned beaver kits were usually found. We were going to have to go through the charade of pretending someone in Vermont found this orphaned beaver. This is, in fact, what had originally happened, only I was going to report it a year later. The important thing was that Jelly was coming home, which is what the VDFW's game wardens sought to arrange all along.

When I did pick up Jelly, I immediately noticed that she had huge "bug eyes," or eyes that protruded prominently from their sockets. Jelly's mom told me she had always looked like that, even as a little kit. This feature, along with her dark brown coat, easily distinguished her from BK. In addition, Jelly's mom showed me, on her iPhone, pictures of Jelly's outdoor enclosure, where she had to wrangle the beaver out of her lodge and into a carrier. The enclosure was a ten-by-twenty-foot "cuboid," half on land and half in the water, with dog kennel panels on the sides and chain-link fabric underneath and overhead. Jelly's mom told me that she got the plans for the enclosure from Beaver Lady, who had a bunch of such enclosures in her big pond, where she might have as many as thirty beavers at any one time! Tending to them all was apparently Beaver Lady's full-time job. We agreed Beaver Lady was a legend among us beaver rehabbers. I wondered if I could build a similar enclosure for BK?

On the way home with Jelly, I decided to call her Mrs. Beaver. She was no longer Jelly without Bean (I really hated those cute pet names anyway), and Laura and I had already decided that Beaverette #3 was the one for BK. She was healthy, she was a female, she was the same age as BK. Perhaps it was a little premature, but Beaverette #3 could now be considered a married beaver, a Mrs., while Beaverette #2 was still unmated, a Miss. All this could possibly change if BK and Mrs. Beaver really could not get along and Miss Beaver recovered fully from her wounds. But all the signs seemed to be pointing in Mrs. Beaver's direction, and it also took some of the timing pressure off Miss Beaver's recovery.

When I got back home, I weighed Mrs. Beaver in at twenty-three pounds—fifteen pounds lighter than BK, who was still at thirty-eight pounds. I put her downstairs, on the smaller side of the enclosure where BK had been when we had tried to introduce him to Pumpkin. But when I opened the carrier, Mrs. Beaver wouldn't come out. Part of the reason may have been that BK was, literally, having a hissy fit: He waddled back and forth, back and forth, on his side of the enclosure, hissing and hissing at this new arrival. Two hours later, Mrs. Beaver was still in the carrier. She wouldn't come out! So we decided to force her to face the world. I tipped the carrier down, but she was clinging for dear life. Eventually, I had to tip the carrier all the way upside down and shake it a bit before Mrs. Beaver plopped out.

Strangely, she went right to BK and the railing divider, but he hissed at her, and she shied away before coming into direct contact. Then she plopped down by the railing facing him, waiting. She clearly wanted to make friends, but he wasn't having it. BK hissed, waddled back and forth, chewed on the railing bars a bit, and even rattled the chains that he seemed to know kept the gate closed. Eventually, he went off in a huff and got into his large tank for a quick swim before coming right out again to continue his temper tantrum. Was he having flashbacks from his time with Pumpkin, who was in reality a rival male? We took Mrs. Beaver's towel from the carrier, on which she had lain and pooed on her way here, and threw it into BK's side of the enclosure to see if we could get him used to her scent. He was in the large tank again, but he jumped right out and came over to the towel. He smelled it all over and then went over to Mrs. Beaver, hissed at her, and went to smell the towel again. Meanwhile, Mrs. Beaver was patiently waiting for BK to come to his senses.

The next day, we tried to get Mrs. Beaver to use her small metal tank, since we didn't know if she had ever used a water tank before. In the night she had done some solid poos on the concrete floor, as well as some pee, which we picked up with paper towels. But even though I tried twice—once in the morning and again in the evening—to cajole Mrs. Beaver up the ramp into the small metal tank, she flopped out as soon as I put her in. The second time, she also did some loose poo or diarrhea on the ramp, as well as some pee on the concrete floor, which we again had to clean up. I wiped up Mrs. Beaver's pee with an old saddle pad, which I then threw into BK's side to try again to get him used to her smell. BK was intrigued by it and seemed to squat over it, perhaps to deposit his castoreum. Another complication was that, when Laura got into Mrs. Beaver's side of the enclosure to help clean up, Mrs. Beaver suddenly started wagging her tail and lunging at Laura as if she might attack her! Laura got out of there, and I had to clean everything on my own.

Finally, we decided to also put in the shallower plastic tub and filled it with only about a one-inch layer of water on the bottom. I then picked Mrs. Beaver up and put her in and held her down until she drank a little and saw it was only water. I also petted her to let her know she was all right. Later, she went exploring around her enclosure and got into her house with the fur-lined pad and then even got into the plastic tub on her own and drank some water. This was a real breakthrough. I no longer had to worry about Mrs. Beaver staying hydrated; on the other hand, she began imitating BK by chewing on the bars of her railing and investigating weak points for getting out of her enclosure. Now we had two beavers chewing and pushing on the railings, making twice as much noise to keep us up at night! Meanwhile, BK was mostly ignoring Mrs. Beaver and was not hissing at her as often. This still seemed a long way from beaver love, and I wondered if I would ever get them to mate.

As we worked our way through May, Mrs. Beaver adjusted to life in our basement. She now spent all her time in the small metal tank. Before I couldn't get her to stay in, now I couldn't get her out! Even when I drained the tank and filled it again, she stayed inside, impatiently waiting for the water. Mrs. Beaver was doing some good chewing on the willow sticks we gave her, completely denuding them of bark. We also introduced her to Mazuri Rodent Chow nuggets, which now she couldn't get enough of, and this was supplemented by the occasional apple or carrot treat. Mrs. Beaver also began talking to me in her "aaaya" voice, which was of a lower timber than BK's. Laura was convinced she liked me more, which was the opposite of what her New Hampshire mom had told me—namely, that she liked women more than men.

Mrs. Beaver still seemed to like BK, or at least *wanted* to like him. One time, she stuck her nose out through the railing bars into BK's space, as if inviting him to touch noses, and another time she stretched her whole paw and forearm out through the bars toward BK, as if she was reaching out to him, but all he did was hiss at her. Yet there were a couple hopeful signs from BK. For instance, a few times he shared all his belongings—Lynx Toy, Beaver Toy, Horse Pad, and Starry Night Blanket—with Mrs. Beaver, stuffing them through the bars of the railing divider, as if inviting her to smell his scent. Another time he did go nose to nose with her through the bars with nary a hiss, even though in the very next moment they shied away from each other again. Maybe this was progress, of a sort.

In the last week of May, we decided to try putting the two together, after two and a half weeks of living separately side by side. At first, we switched their enclosures, putting BK in Mrs. Beaver's side with the small metal tank (we took out the small plastic tub, which we knew he'd chew on) and putting Mrs. Beaver in BK's side with the large tank. We hoped this would get them used to each other's smells. But all BK wanted to do was move Mrs. Beaver's chewed sticks back over to her (formerly his) side of the enclosure. Although he managed to flop into the small tank, he barely fit in there now, the displaced water slopping over the sides onto the floor. Meanwhile, it took a lot of coaxing and corralling to get Mrs. Beaver to go up the wooden gangplank and down the Beavertail into the large tank. Once she was in, she happily swam around and dipped and dived the whole length of the tank. In the evening, when we switched the beavers back, I noticed some brown liquid at the back of the dog crate on Mrs. Beaver's side of the enclosure. Apparently, BK, while he was on her side, had marked the crate as his territory with his castoreum.

Three days before the end of the month, we decided to open the divider railings for the first time and let BK and Mrs. Beaver share one big enclosure. Part of our motivation behind this was selfish: The incessant chewing and ear-splitting screeches as both beavers chewed and pushed on their railings, scraping them across the concrete floor, was driving us crazy! Laura had to sleep in the living room because they made too much noise, since our bedroom was directly above them in the basement. It was either put them together or move them outside!

I decked myself out like a hockey goalie, wearing muck boots and thick leather gloves and armed with a sponge mop. The two beavers encountered each other several times. Once they body slammed each other on their sides, and BK charged at Mrs. Beaver, but there was no biting. Eventually Mrs. Beaver gave up trying to be friendly and shied away from BK every time he came near or else she lay very still, trying not to be noticed. While we were filling the large tank, BK got in first and swam around in the shallow water and then got out. Then Mrs. Beaver got in and swam around for a while. We put the railings back up and locked BK in the small tank side of the enclosure. At least no one got hurt.

We repeated this ritual of opening the divider railings and letting the beavers explore each other's spaces a few more times. Mostly the beavers stayed out of each other's way, although BK charged Mrs. Beaver when she appeared to threaten Laura by pushing her shoulder against Laura's leg to get her out of her space! For some reason, BK liked to soak in the small metal tank while Mrs. Beaver stretched her legs in the large one, even doing somersaults and rolls like an otter. At the end of each day, we put the divider railings back up again. The last time we did this, BK was back on his own side of the enclosure with the large tank, while Mrs. Beaver was with the small one. BK marked his blanket and furry pad with his castoreum, leaving a distinct oily smear, which I took and spread onto Mrs. Beaver's back, hoping this might trick BK into accepting her by smelling his own scent!

Nonetheless, I was beginning to despair of ever getting these two to mate. I called Beaver Lady and she advised that I never put them together without supervising them, as a rehabber in a similar situation came into her enclosure one day to find the smaller beaver dead at the hands of the larger one. She said that usually a young male and female beaver became playmates almost right away, wrestling and grooming each other. Since it was still possible that Jelly's mom got her sex wrong, I took Mrs. Beaver to our vet to be x-rayed. This confirmed Mrs. Beaver was indeed a female.

Finally, at 1:30 A.M. on the third day of June, I was woken by a lot of chewing on the bars and scraping and screeching of railings being pushed and shoved across the concrete. Laura called me downstairs. Both BK and Mrs. Beaver were on the same side (her side) of the enclosure! Mrs. Beaver was in the small tank, and BK was chewing on some willow sticks nearby. But the divider railing was still intact! Indeed, the two railings that we used as a gate to open the entire enclosure were still chained securely together. How did the beavers get together? It was a mystery.

I shepherded BK back to his own side of the enclosure, him protesting all the while, and chained the railings together. But lo and behold, later that same morning, at 5:30 A.M., I found the two beavers together again! This time they were on BK's side of the enclosure, and Mrs. Beaver was lying on the SAME pad as BK. I was half afraid that BK had killed her and she was dead, just as

Beaver Lady told me might happen. But then Mrs. Beaver lifted her hind paw and started scratching her belly. She also lifted her head, and I knew she was fine. Later that morning, I found them snuggled up next to each other. Mrs. Beaver was even grooming BK and using his body as a pillow for her head. The beavers had taken matters into their own hands and decided they wanted to be together after all, despite my best efforts to keep them apart!

At least I solved the mystery of how the beavers got together. The first time, one or both of the beavers must have lifted the railing enough that BK could crawl underneath to Mrs. Beaver's side of the enclosure. The second time, they had undone the chain lashing two railings together at the bottom, since the chain and its double-ended snap were missing. The railings could then be pried apart enough that Mrs. Beaver slipped through to join BK. Where was the chain now? The beavers had carried it off and hidden it somewhere, no doubt to prevent me from ever chaining them apart again! I surrendered to the beavers' will and simply opened the entire enclosure.

Biology is a powerful thing.

5

Stream Time

Now that BK and Mrs. Beaver were mated, they never slept apart. Every time I came downstairs to the basement in the morning, I would find them lying side by side on the pad, often with Mrs. Beaver resting her head on BK's back, using it as a pillow. They swam together in the large tank, swimming around each other in circles and sometimes chasing each other back and forth the length of the tank. If BK still chased or charged Mrs. Beaver, it now seemed half-hearted and mostly in play. Any hissing and body slamming that remained was over food. For example, two days after the beavers got together, Laura fed Mrs. Beaver some kale while BK was swimming in the large tank, but he immediately came out, wanting his own treat. At first BK tried to push Mrs. Beaver off her kale by bodychecking her with his shoulder, but Mrs. Beaver quickly retaliated by slapping BK in the face with her tail! They ended up happily nibbling on their own kale stalks, courtesy of Laura.

In mid-June, Laura and I watched BK and Mrs. Beaver wrestle each other for the first time. At first, BK used his superior weight to push Mrs. Beaver backward. But Mrs. Beaver was strong, and soon it was she who was pushing BK back across the floor! The match was over when BK ducked his head and stalked off, raising the white flag in surrender. Mrs. Beaver eventually became rather bossy, perhaps sensing that BK was a big, fat pushover. About a week after their first wrestling match, for example, Laura fed an apple to BK but Mrs. Beaver took it away from him. When Laura gave another apple to BK, he took it into the large water tank to eat undisturbed in his own special way—by nibbling all the skin off first before eating the flesh underneath. Mrs. Beaver was also bossy in the water. When she was on the lower part of the Beavertail ramp or even swimming near it, BK had to belly flop off the upper part, making a big splash in the water! She was a more agile swimmer than BK, so she could chase him all around, sometimes even climbing up onto his back. He could not escape her, even when he dived under the Beavertail ramp into the far end of the tank, which was harder for BK to do because he had more fat and therefore floated more easily. Mrs. Beaver was, in fact, quite a water baby, spending most of her time in the tank. She got in even as we were draining or just starting to fill the tank and had taken the ramp down, since she was able to climb on top of the sticks piled by the ramp and drop in.

There were also exquisitely tender moments between BK and Mrs. Beaver. One day, when BK was swimming inside the tank and Mrs. Beaver was just outside it, she reached up to the edge of the tank and, at the same time, so did he from inside, and they touched noses. There was also the time when, as I was filling the large tank, they were on the rubber mat just beside the tank, grooming each other in a "69" position, with BK nibbling on the base of Mrs. Beaver's tail and she nibbling on the base of his tail. I watched them play Beaver Wrestle at least three more times in June after their first match. Always they wrestled just as I was draining or filling the large tank, once even wrestling right underneath me as I was trying to do my work. Sometimes BK won these matches, but usually Mrs. Beaver, who seemed to have a greater ratio of muscle to fat than BK, was able to push him back in the end. I was just thankful BK had found someone else to wrestle with. Occasionally, though, BK would grab my arm and push against me, perhaps for variety, even if Mrs. Beaver never did so.

At the end of June, BK had an accident that gave us quite a scare. It happened as I was filling the large tank after having drained and cleaned it, and I had put the ramp back up so the beavers could get back in. While I was upstairs, I suddenly heard a big splash! I came down to find BK getting out of the tank and limping a little bit. Laura and I noticed some blood on his right hind foot. After Laura coaxed him onto her lap, I examined his foot and found that he had torn the toenail off the third toe. BK's toenails were long, and I suspect he had caught it in one of the metal perforations on the Beavertail ramp. A few days ago, I had seen him catch it there, as well, but that time without incident. On the advice of my vet, we sprinkled cornstarch on the bleeding toe and then wrapped it in two socks, the first a long tube sock and then a little bootie sock over that. Each time, I also poured cornstarch into the socks before putting them on BK's foot. We then wrapped the toe and upper part of the foot in vet wrap to put some pressure on the wound. That seemed to stabilize it. We put BK in the dog crate for the night, first putting in his pad and a towel over that. I then put in his bowl of nuggets. He was not happy, chewing at the bars, wanting out. So I put some towels over the crate to make it dark to hopefully keep him quiet. That seemed to do the trick, as he commenced eating his nuggets.

The next day I installed a car mat on the lower part of the ramp, just as I had done on the upper part last December, so neither beaver could get hurt on it anymore. Laura and I also examined BK's foot—which was challenging because one of us had to hold BK still while the other grabbed his foot to inspect the afflicted toe—and it looked a lot better. The bleeding had stopped and scabbed over. I applied some Vetericyn and consulted with the vet, who advised BK didn't need antibiotics and that his nail would probably grow back. That evening, Laura and I had to convince BK to get back in the water, since he hadn't been in since the accident. Laura was able to coax him over to the ramp and then up the ramp to the top of the Beavertail. But then BK was hesitant to go down the Beavertail, where he'd hurt himself. Eventually, with our encouragement, he got in, drank a bunch of water, and did a big poo. As he was in the water and later when he got out, he sniffed the air, perhaps checking for whatever scary predator had ripped off his toenail. Later, when I drained the tank, I found the toenail. I've kept it to this day, and I'm holding it now as I write this.

BK's accident encouraged me to complete the outdoor enclosure I'd been working on the entire month. Plans for the enclosure came from Jelly's mom, who in turn had gotten it from Beaver Lady. It consisted of a dog kennel, which I had ordered online, that enclosed a ten-by-twenty-foot area and was six feet high, half of which (one hundred square feet) was on land and half in the water. I also got some coated chain-link fabric, which I stitched together to make a continuous barrier on the floor of the enclosure, both on land and in the water, so the beavers could not get out. I also put another chain-link barrier on the roof of the enclosure, so no predator—whether they be fishers, bobcats, or even bears—could climb up and get in. The chain-link fabric—which consisted of three rolls each five feet wide—had to be stitched together to make a continuous barrier on the floor and roof of the enclosure. It was an incredibly laborious process: The fabric had knuckle selvage, which meant I had to crouch down onto the fabric and undo each knuckle of one roll with a pair of pliers and then reclose the knuckle over a wire strand on the opposite fabric. Then, I had to "weave" the opposing knuckle onto a strand from the original fabric. This took me untold hours—working hunched over every day for the first two weeks of the month—to complete. Once the kennel panels arrived, Laura and I assembled them onto the fabric—half in the water and half out—and I then stitched the fabric to the panels, using clamps and rolls of thin coated wire, which took me until the end of the month to finish.

By mid-July, I was ready to put the beavers into their new outdoor enclosure! This couldn't have come soon enough, because, with both beavers using the large tank, we had to change the water every day. Moreover, I kept having to replace the sump pump, because, unless I stored it far away, the beavers were able to reach through the bars of the railing and pull both the electric cord and the drain hose into the enclosure, which they then proceeded to chew to bits.

We prepped their new home by putting in the Dogloo lined with a furry pad, some fresh towels, their Starry

Night Blanket, a dish full of nuggets, and some freshly cut poplar saplings. We carried BK out first in his large carrier, which Laura and I had to do together as he was so heavy! Laura stayed with him while I went back and corralled Mrs. Beaver into the smaller carrier and carried her out. When we finally had the beavers together, we opened both carriers at the same time. Both BK and Mrs. Beaver explored on land for a little bit before Mrs. Beaver got into the water, then BK. BK was more familiar with this environment, as this had been his Swimway, where he had swum laps last year. Mrs. Beaver, on the other hand, spent several minutes hiding underwater, which led me to suspect she was almost shell shocked. Eventually, however, they both became more confident and relaxed in their new surroundings. They began swimming around and wrestled in the water, with Mrs. Beaver at one point pushing BK against the kennel sides like in a cage wrestling match! I found it very gratifying to see them enjoying their new enclosure after all the hard work I had put into making it.

It was a pity the weather had to ruin it all. For the first five days, the beavers were allowed to settle into their new home: They'd sleep the mornings away in the Dogloo, then emerge to eat nuggets, play Beaver Wrestle in the water, move sticks around, or throw their wet bedding out of the house to alert housekeeping it was time to change it! But on the third Sunday of July, it rained all day. Naturally, the water level in the stream rose and remained high all that day and into the next. In one sense, this was great for the beavers, because they now had a nice, deep pool to swim and play in. BK did some flips in the water, like an otter, while Mrs. Beaver at one point hitched a ride on BK's back as he swam around. They also played Beaver Wrestle in the deep water and in other ways cavorted happily together.

But then, two days later, a thunderstorm rolled in around 8:00 p.m., which included a burst of heavy rain. This raised the water level, already high, so much that the quiet little stream now became a raging torrent. It swept the entire beaver enclosure twenty feet downstream and turned it almost ninety degrees sideways! Fortunately the enclosure ran aground on a sandbar on the opposite bank, where it was perched precariously with shallow water rushing all around and through. I prayed that it would go no farther, because I knew that downstream there were some large rocks and boulders that might crush the enclosure with the beavers inside.

I had never felt so helpless. Laura and I stood on our side of the bank, not daring to even attempt to cross what we could lightly skip and splash through just a day or two ago. The water was angry and it would swiftly sweep us to our deaths if we so much as dipped a toe in its roaring current. All we could do was shine our flashlight in the direction of the enclosure, where we caught a glimpse of the beavers, stranded in a giant cage that, somehow, was still intact. I honestly didn't know how I'd react if BK and Mrs. Beaver were swept downstream. All that work, all that care, all that love that we put into bringing up BK would be gone. It would be like losing a child.

We called out to BK and Mrs. Beaver, and BK heard us, for he answered our call with his own "aaaya" cry. He then stood up on his hind legs in the southwest corner of the enclosure, which was nearest to us, and lifted a paw in the air, as if trying to reach out to us. Tears streaming down our faces, Laura and I called out to him, telling him that he would be OK, we would rescue him and Mrs. Beaver in the morning. We spent a sleepless night checking on the beavers every few hours. By the early morning, the water level had gone down enough that the worst danger was past and we would be able to get across the stream and evacuate the beavers at first light. I even saw one of the beavers go into the Dogloo for shelter and perhaps a bit of sleep.

As soon as there was enough daylight to see by, we evacuated the beavers from the enclosure, as the water had gone down almost to normal level and we could get across. Physically, the beavers seemed to be unharmed by the whole experience. As soon as we got them downstairs in our basement, we filled up the large water tank. Mrs. Beaver got in right away, but BK went up the ramp and then turned around and went back down. He laid out flat on the rubber stall mat right underneath the stairs, like a rug. I went to pet him but he hissed at me, telling me to leave him alone: He was tired and was going to rest now. Later in the day, I saw BK swimming in the tank with Mrs. Beaver, the two swimming, as they often did, back to front around each other and egging each other on as they did rolls and somersaults in the water. I also saw them outside the tank playing Beaver Wrestle, so I knew they were back to feeling somewhat normal and safe. We gave them nuggets and brought in some of the leafy willow sticks that they had out in the enclosure.

Four days after the Big Storm, I held a Beaver Enclosure Move Party. Including me and Laura, we had ten pairs of hands to wrangle the beast: friends, neighbors, family, and members of Protect Our Wildlife (POW), an advocacy group on whose board I sat. One person was stationed at each of the four corners of the enclosure, and one at each of the six metal posts that bisected each ten-foot panel. At a cue, we all lifted together and slowly walked the enclosure back to the original stream bed and then swung it ninety degrees to its original position. To make the enclosure more secure, I lashed the upstream panel to two pine trees growing on either bank of the stream with metal cables.

After the enclosure was in place, everyone wanted to see the beavers move back in and enjoy what we had all worked so hard to achieve. Laura carried out BK, then I carried out Mrs. Beaver, who was more reluctant to leave the large tank. By the time Mrs. Beaver and I arrived, BK was already in the water. She sniffed the enclosure on the land side before daring to go into the water and play Beaver Wrestle with BK. But soon Mrs. Beaver got agitated with all the unfamiliar people watching, and she began taking her aggression out on BK, chasing him all around the enclosure. We left them alone and all enjoyed a cup of my homemade hard cider while sitting around, swapping wildlife and wilderness stories.

The only other exciting thing to happen in July was that, in the last week of the month, I got to witness what I believe was beaver sex. I had just given the beavers some nuggets and swapped their wet sleeping pad with a dry one when I saw something odd going on in the southwest corner of the enclosure, which lay in the stream. BK was lying on top of Mrs. Beaver and seemed to be holding her head under water! His tail was positioned off to the side from hers. Mrs. Beaver was obviously holding her breath, for her head was under water for several minutes; then she came up for air and put it back down again. If this was beaver sex, I don't think this kind of lovemaking—which seemed to involve waterboarding as foreplay!—would translate well to humans. This heightened sexual activity was confirmed on the last day of July, when Mrs. Beaver grew more jealous of Laura than usual. She drove Laura out of the enclosure and then, letting her vulva emerge from her cloaca, dragged it on the ground, marking her territory against all female competitors for BK's attention, regardless of species!

August was a quiet month, except for a couple of times when we brought the beavers back to the basement for fear of approaching storms. We called these "Evacuation Drills." If I objected to these drills, preferring to adopt a wait-and-see attitude, Laura played the guilt card and asked if I wanted the beavers to die. Well, of course I didn't, so we did the drills. The reason I objected was because it was now getting harder to evacuate the beavers. Mrs. Beaver was now at thirty-three pounds, having gained a whole ten pounds in just three months of being with us! BK was still at thirty-eight pounds, but Mrs. Beaver was gaining on him!

The other reason I didn't want to evacuate the beavers was because we'd have to drain and fill the large water tank again. That was the great advantage of the beavers being in the stream: It was self-cleansing. Yet both BK and Mrs. Beaver loved the large water tank, and they grew impatient when I had to change the water every day. After I drained it, the beavers would flatten themselves on the stall mats, looking so dejected! As soon as I started filling the tank, they would get back in and float side by side until the water was deep enough to do their whoop-de-dos, rolls, and wheelies.

Our first drill in the second week of the month ended being a big nothingburger. But the second, just five days later, was justified. We were getting the remnants of Tropical Storm Fred, and it rained all day—not a torrential downpour, but a steady, light rain. Nonetheless, this caused the stream to jump its bank and encroach upon the ground almost to the entrance to the Dogloo at the far northeast corner. This meant that the enclosure was almost entirely flooded, and the beavers might have been sleeping in the wet if they had remained outside. At least the enclosure, held in place by the guy-wires secured to the trees, was not swept away downstream.

I took advantage of the beavers' absence from the enclosure to repair some gaps in the chain-link fabric, especially the part submerged in the water, which the beavers seemed to be chewing on. The first time I tried this, the beavers were with me in the enclosure. BK left off eating his Rodent Chow nuggets, which I hoped would distract him, and dove into the water and swam over to me. He clearly saw that I was hard at work on something and wanted to help. Mostly this involved him floating in front of me to keep me company as I sat waist-deep in the water in my bathing suit. Since his big, fat body was directly over my hands, I ended up having to feel my way along the fabric, testing for any stray jagged ends of wire. This ended up being the best way to do the repair work!

In September, things got exciting again. On just the second day of the month, Laura came out in the early morning to find the enclosure empty, both beavers gone!

I was not at home, as every morning and afternoon I left
for about two hours to drive kids to and from school as a
part-time bus driver. Despite my repairs, the beavers had
managed to chew the chain-link fabric and make a hole
large enough to squeeze through. This was in the southwest corner of the enclosure in the stream, which, perhaps
not coincidentally, was where I caught the beavers having
sex. Mrs. Beaver had stuck around and Laura found her
on the bank by the enclosure. But BK had wandered off.
Laura put Mrs. Beaver back inside the enclosure, but she
just got out again through the hole! Fortunately she came
right back to Laura, thinking she had nuggets. When I
arrived back home, I heard Laura calling to me, frantically,
to bring a carrier. I found her holding down Mrs. Beaver by
the scruff, the folds of fur and fat just behind her front legs.
Mrs. Beaver wasn't happy with Laura, that's for sure—she
had been held there for the past half hour—and Laura
was terrified she was going to get a second beaver bite,
this time from Mrs. Beaver. Together we managed to get
Mrs. Beaver into the carrier, and I brought her back downstairs to the basement, where I filled the large tank for her.

But BK was gone. I searched upstream as far as I could
go before encountering impenetrably thick underbrush,
but no BK. Then I searched downstream, peeking into the
neighbor's pond and going down to the swimming hole,
but no BK. Laura even went to the southern border of our
property, about half a mile down the road, and worked

her way downstream, but no BK. She checked the enclosure every half hour to see if he had returned, but no BK. Was he really gone? Was he actually hiding somewhere close by? Was it too much to hope that he'd come back and was simply exploring, perhaps sowing his oats? Laura could hardly believe BK would leave his mate and seemed especially offended by his apparent abandonment of Mrs. Beaver. It was like a large hole had bored its way into both our hearts. Imagine if your child went off to college one day and never said goodbye!

But, in the end, BK did come back! Just after Laura finished teaching her last horseback riding lesson at 5:30 P.M., she found him swimming in the stream just south of the enclosure, where he used to swim laps in the Swimway. She enticed him out of the water with an apple and a carrot and wrestled him into the large carrier, even though he squawked in complaint. She then brought him downstairs, and when I came home from my afternoon bus run, I saw BK and Mrs. Beaver lying side by side on blankets by the water tank. It was as if BK had never left at all! But Laura was still indignant that BK had left Mrs. Beaver. How could he have abandoned his mate like that? Did he not love her at all?! I stuck up for BK. Perhaps, I argued, BK intended to come back all along: He was simply scouting out a place for them both to settle in, where they could dam the stream and build a lodge. Perhaps Mrs. Beaver understood this, too, content to wait for her man and keep the home fires burning. We'd never know the exact dynamics of their relationship.

The next week, a newspaper reporter and a photographer came to do a story about my beavers rehabbing in their unique outdoor enclosure. It was imperative that I fix the hole where the beavers got out before the reporter came; it would be embarrassing to show her an enclosure with no beavers! Fortunately, I got a lead on two ten-by-six-foot panels made of galvanized chain-link fence that looked to be of a heavier grade than the fabric, and therefore harder for beavers to chew through. They could simply be superimposed over the hole and, indeed, almost all of the fabric that was underwater. Laura and I spent a whole day doing this work, and just barely managed to bring the beavers back to the enclosure before the reporter arrived! The beavers seemed grateful to swim in fresh stream water again. I was grateful I didn't have to change their water, nor listen to BK pushing on the railing, making those ear-splitting scraping sounds of metal on concrete! Best of all, the reporter seemed suitably impressed by the enclosure, and the beavers within it. They took a photo of me posing next to the enclosure while the beavers swam in the stream. I explained to the reporter that BK and Mrs. Beaver each had an assigned job within their "marriage." BK's was to build dams, which he did by jamming sticks, leaves, and grass against the downstream side of the dog kennel panels, making their stream deeper.

Mrs. Beaver's job was to build a lodge, which she also had done during her time as Jelly with her previous rehabber in New Hampshire. Since there already was a Dogloo, Mrs. Beaver simply added to it by jamming sticks under and over the existing structure.

However, fame, as the saying goes, has a way of biting you in the ass. Just five days after the reporter's visit, we received a second visitor: an enforcement officer from the Vermont Department of Environmental Conservation (DEC). Their job, among other things, is to manage water resources and enforce the rules and regulations thereof. The officer arrived in the early afternoon, knocking on the door. Laura was alone, as I was on my afternoon bus run. The officer asked to see our enclosure based on a formal written complaint lodged with the department. Laura asked who the complainant was, but the officer refused to divulge this information until he completed his investigation.

Laura showed the officer the enclosure. BK and Mrs. Beaver were swimming in the stream. Immediately they tail-slapped the water in alarm when the strange officer showed up. The first words out of the officer's mouth were, "You're going to have to remove this enclosure immediately. It's a prohibited discharge as specified in Statute 1259a." Laura asked how, specifically, the enclosure could be classified as a "discharge." The officer rattled off a list of "issues" with the enclosure being in state waters: It was

inhibiting the "the free passage" of fish and human kayakers; it could wash downstream and damage the intake
dam of the state Fish Hatchery; it collected debris; and it
was allowing the beavers to excrete their waste into the
water. Laura rebutted these objections point-by-point:
The fish were small minnows who could easily pass through
the wire mesh; this portion of the stream was only a foot
deep, hardly enough to accommodate kayakers; the state
Fish Hatchery was more than a mile downstream, and
even during the big summer storm in July the enclosure
only moved a few feet; debris in the enclosure was put there
by BK building his dam, and when released the beavers
would build a dam upstream anyway; beavers were naturally part of the landscape, and they and plenty of other
animals poop in the water. The officer responded that
beavers were a "nuisance"; he was authorized to remove
any dam less than three years old deemed to be a threat to
infrastructure downstream; and in the past, he had trapped
and killed many beavers. Finally, Laura asked if there was
any way to request a special permit to have the enclosure in
the water. The officer responded that he was always asked
that question, and the answer was always no. The department did not want to set any precedent.

After the officer left, Laura had a good cry. She was
still upset when I came home, and she told me all that
had transpired. She said she now understood how parents
felt when Social Services were called to investigate their

parenting. She, too, was afraid the state would confiscate our wards, if we did not fix our "problem."

The next day, I talked to the DEC enforcement officer over the phone. He told me many of the same things that he had told Laura, including that I was in violation of Statute 1259a, banning discharges into state waters, and my enclosure was classified as a solid "discharge"; he was concerned about the dog kennel panels washing downstream, since he had read in a Facebook post about how POW helped move back my enclosure after it washed downstream during a storm; and there was no possible permit for discharges, even though I was willing to make modifications to be more in compliance. But I had one more card up my sleeve to play.

"What about underwater traps that trappers use to trap and kill beavers? Those are also metal contraptions in the water not so different from my enclosure. How are these legal and yet not considered 'discharges?'" The officer was flummoxed. He said I had a good point and he would raise it at the department's meeting tomorrow chaired by the commissioner and the general counsel. He praised me for being so "reasonable." Most residents in Roxbury, he explained, were "difficult" to deal with, and occasionally violent. "One time I even had a gun stuck in my face!" What I didn't tell him was that, if he or anyone in his department came for my beavers, he'd be staring down the barrel of my .22!

Our conversation ended with the officer informing me that his boss, the chief environmental enforcement officer, would be calling next week to tell me what was decided at the department meeting. I felt compelled to inform him, in return, that he and his department could expect to see themselves in the news after I updated the reporter about their visit. After I hung up the phone, I had a sudden wave of déjà vu. It felt like the beavers and their parents (meaning Laura and I) were being called in to the principal's office for a conference about their behavior at school. But it still wasn't clear what, exactly, any of us had done wrong.

In the meantime, I was also busy that summer playing matchmaker for Miss Beaver, who was still all alone in the outdoor enclosure behind the house. I called Pumpkin's mom on the off chance she would be open to pairing her ward with mine (a female confirmed by x-ray!). It turned out she was very enthusiastic about the match. It was arranged: I would bring Miss Beaver down to her place in southern Vermont on Sunday, June 20.

It was quite a victory for us to even get to this point. If you recall, I had taken in Miss Beaver back in April when she had been mauled by a dog, and we had been working on healing her wounds and rehabbing her injured muscles ever since. It was slow going. In the second week of May, we took her back to the vet for another shot of Convenia, and the vet had to drain a large swelling at the base of her tail, full of pus, which spurted out in a steady stream of yellow, foul-smelling liquid like a fire hose. We then put Miss Beaver on the floor to observe her movements. Although she was able to hobble back to the carrier, demonstrating she could move her legs, she never moved her tail. The vet said if she still couldn't move that, she couldn't be released, because beavers use their tails to steady themselves while swimming in the water.

For the rest of May and into June, we'd take Miss Beaver out from the enclosure, put her in the outdoor plastic garden pool full of warm water, and then put her on a towel on the ground in order to flush her wounds with Betadine scrub. We'd do this at least three, sometimes four times a day. As her wounds began to heal, even as smaller, hidden ones kept revealing themselves when they erupted pus, Miss Beaver made steady progress in her physical therapy. One sign of this was her greater mobility in the water. She began swimming around, doing dips and dives, and we even observed her moving her tail! This was more than confirmed for us one day when Laura attempted to pick her up out of the water, and she splashed her with it! We were so relieved because it meant we wouldn't have to put her down; she could be released.

But Miss Beaver was also becoming more mobile on land. At least three times we put her in the pool and then went to do other chores, such as turning out the horses, on the assumption that she couldn't get out on her own.

But when we came back, she was gone! The first two times she was walking to the stream, but she came back when we called her. We took that as a sign that Miss Beaver, despite all her complaining at our ministrations, recognized, on some level, that we were trying to help and that she trusted us. But the third time, we almost lost her for good. Miss Beaver didn't come back when Laura called; instead, it seemed she was ready to be on her own, for she had well and truly disappeared. Eventually, Laura found her at the far northeastern corner of our property, where our little stream drained into the much larger Flint Brook. Miss Beaver was on the rocks, just about to go into the water, when Laura reached out and plucked her back. If she had gotten into the water, she would have entered her element and swum beyond our reach forever. Even though Miss Beaver hissed and struggled as Laura carried her back, it was for her own good: She wasn't quite ready to be released yet, whatever she thought to the contrary.

On the day of her big trip down south to her new home, we loaded Miss Beaver into a carrier after putting her in the pool for a last drink and poo. The trip took me two hours. Miss Beaver was quiet the whole time, except at the end when she finally lost patience and I could hear her chewing on the carrier. When we arrived, I carried Miss Beaver to the ground floor of a barn-like house, where in a corner by the door was Pumpkin's enclosure, a rather small space but with a water tank the same size as ours wedged into the far side. Pumpkin himself came out of a shelter made from a wide board roof with a piece of fabric across the front. We put the carrier in with him, and almost immediately Miss Beaver poked her face out from the rear left side of the carrier! The sounds I had heard was her chewing through the rear plastic ventilation grill until the hole was big enough that she could stick her whole face, if not her whole body, out of the carrier. Pumpkin and Miss Beaver gingerly sniffed each other, until he went around to the front gate of the carrier, perhaps to get a better view and sniff. After about fifteen minutes, we decided to let Miss Beaver out. Pumpkin's mom was sitting inside the enclosure in her bare feet, which made me a little nervous, but I was armed with my rake. Miss Beaver ambled out, with Pumpkin keeping his distance, hissing a little but not charging or going to attack her. She settled in a corner of the enclosure. I showed Pumpkin's mom her remaining wounds and where to flush them and how she might have to be put into the water if she couldn't figure out the ramp right away. Pumpkin then went into the water and almost immediately came out again to cuddle with his mom, who playfully put her finger right into his mouth, against his teeth, just as I did with BK. After spending an hour there, I left, with a last goodbye to Miss Beaver and a promise to stay in touch. The next I heard of Miss Beaver was in September, when I read in an article Pumpkin's mom wrote for the local newspaper that Pumpkin and "Pye" (her new nickname) were now an inseparable couple, and they were to settle in for the winter in a neighbor's pond, surrounded by a wire fence. I called Pumpkin's mom and arranged to visit Miss Beaver at her new home sometime soon. It felt good to have a happy ending, especially after all the stress of having to deal with the DEC over BK and Mrs. Beaver's enclosure.

But beavers weren't the only mammals I rehabbed that summer. In June I received an orphaned baby least weasel, found in someone's driveway in Wolcott, who was about three to four weeks old and just starting to open one of its eyes. At this stage, he would be weaning off milk and starting to eat solid food, so I fed him a transition mixture of A/D wet cat food, kitten milk formula, and Missing Link supplement, feeding him a couple cc's at a time using a canula and syringe, every three hours. (Weasels have similar metabolisms to cats, so we feed them the same milk formulas when young.) He had a tick, white and fat from feeding on his blood, on his right foot that I had to pull off with tweezers. Laura combed through his fur to make sure no other ticks were on him, and we couldn't see any. I settled him in our "incubator," which was the same blue plastic box I had used as a house when we first got BK. When I looked in on him before bed, Baby Weasel was sleeping contentedly, curled between his heating pad and a scrap of mink fur, looking super cute.

For the next three days, I continued to feed Baby Weasel his A/D–milk formula–Missing Link mixture, while Laura managed to find and pull off four or five more ticks. As we held him during feeding times, we found that he had a tickle spot, midway on his belly, which made his hind leg go in circles about a million miles an hour, trying to scratch the itch. He also made "trilling" noises, or what some call "chittering" or "chirping," which apparently is their "contact call" when interacting with fellow weasels in the wild. It was a strangely soothing sound, which I would describe somewhere between a cat's purr and a bird's song.

By the third day, Baby Weasel's other eye had fully opened as well, so he could now eat on his own. I quickly transitioned him to pinkie and small furry mice, his "adult" food. I also transferred him to the large cage I had used for the injured mink back in December, complete with a nest box, two running wheels, a heated water dish, a paper towel roll (to hide in), and some shavings. Baby Weasel immediately made his home in the nest box, which had some fresh mink coat scraps that he loved to curl in, as I found whenever I lifted the lid to check on him.

In July we moved the cage with Baby Weasel up from the basement onto our porch, just outside the sliding door to our bedroom, as the weather was getting warmer and I thought Baby Weasel could use the fresh air. Baby Weasel was growing into an adult and getting much more active. Although we rarely caught a glimpse of him during the day, we always heard him at night when he came out to run in the large exercise wheel, which made a squeaking sound as it went round and round. Both Laura and I were woken around two o'clock every morning when the wheel went squeak, squeak, squeak just outside our bedroom for fifteen to twenty minutes and then went quiet again.

It wasn't until the middle of the month that we finally got to see Baby Weasel exercising during the daytime. His feet were a blur as he was in the wheel, running, running, running, until he jumped out and ran up the cage wall and then leaped onto the top of the wheel, which he then rode down to the ground. It reminded me of when we tickled his tummy when he was younger, making his hind legs go a million miles an hour. Then he repeated this wheel exercise at least five to six times during the time we watched him. He was ready for a live prey test, as he clearly demonstrated his speed and stamina, which would give him an edge in hunting.

It wasn't until the last week of July that I began catching live mice in my small Havahart trap so I could conduct live prey tests on Baby Weasel. The first mouse I caught was rather large—it may not have even been a mouse, but some other kind of rodent—and after chores I put him in Baby Weasel's cage. He was half dead by that stage, but I watched as Baby Weasel sniffed him out, although I didn't see him attack and kill him. When I checked back about half an hour later, the mouse was dead. I couldn't really tell if Baby Weasel had eaten any of it, but I left it in the cage anyway. The next day, the rodent was gone—either eaten or cached away—and I watched as Baby Weasel bounced and leaped all around his cage, climbed the walls, and hung upside down on the roof. He was getting bolder and even more active, no longer skulking behind his nest box or caring if we were watching, and he was certainly not limiting himself to his wheel for exercise. He was also eating well, judging by all the scat on top of his nest box.

Over the next couple of days, Baby Weasel put on the same display, coming out of his nest box even as I was watching, and bopping all around, doing leaps and bounces around the enclosure. Toward the very end of the month, I found two live adult mice in my Havahart trap on separate days, and therefore I was able to conduct two live prey tests. In the first test, when I put the mouse in the cage, the weasel ignored it at first, but the mouse tried to hide behind the nest box and that's where the weasel also hid, so the weasel flushed it out. The mouse was quick, but Baby Weasel was quicker. The mouse fled into the wheel, but Baby Weasel got on top and flushed him out of there. Then the mouse ran up the wire, but Baby Weasel followed him and grabbed him and brought him back down. A few times Baby Weasel tried to kill the mouse but it got away. Eventually, Baby Weasel, by lying on his back, was able to reach up and grab the mouse by its throat and kill it. Thus ended the first live prey test.

In the second live prey test, the mouse really gave Baby Weasel a run for his money. It crawled up the sides of the cage and even onto the roof, and it bounced from end to end at lightning speed, in an effort to get away from Baby Weasel, almost like a ping-pong ball running for its life. At times Baby Weasel didn't even know where the mouse was and seemed distracted, going back to his usual hangout behind the nest box. But then his attention was engaged again by the mouse's movements, and the chase was on once more. I began to wonder when the mouse would tire of running and simply give up, but this went on for a full half hour. At one point Baby Weasel was in the water dish and bit his own hindquarters in his excitement, thinking this was his prey. Eventually, the mouse, perhaps exhausted, no longer went up the sides of the cage but stayed down below, and then it was doomed. Baby Weasel grabbed it and got a stranglehold on its throat as it stretched beside the mouse and killed it. Before I released him, I was going to have to do more live prey testing until I could see Baby Weasel had honed his hunting skills and gotten his kill time down. But then, Baby Weasel may not have been so hungry this time, since I had fed him well last night, and these prey tests may have been about play and the sport of the chase, rather than survival.

It was not until the second week of August that I released Baby Weasel, when he was eleven or twelve weeks old. He was still serenading us at night, exercising furiously on his wheel. I was also able to conduct a final live prey test before his release. This time, I was not on hand to watch the weasel hunt the mouse, as I had to run to the bathroom after depositing the mouse in the cage. But by the time I came back, a few minutes later, the mouse was nowhere to be seen, which meant that Baby Weasel had caught, killed, and cached it in that time, which was pretty fast. Baby Weasel poked his head out and barked at me, perhaps boasting of his latest kill!

On the day of his release, I fed Baby Weasel a last meal of three furry mice in the morning. Then Flower Girl, her husband, her two sons, and her mother came over around 1:30 P.M. to help me release Baby Weasel. Flower Girl's husband and I had to carry the whole cage out from the porch into the back of our truck. He got in the bed with his two boys and held the cage steady while we drove to the edge of the field that bordered our forest. We carried the cage to a rock pile that used to host wild grape vines, which had numerous hidey-holes for Baby Weasel in the gaps between the rocks. When we opened the lid of the cage, Baby Weasel made a great leap into the air and landed flat on his back, but wouldn't come out. So we tipped the cage gently onto its side, making sure the nest box, behind which Baby Weasel was still trying to hide, didn't crush him. Baby Weasel then ran out, not into the rock pile as I had hoped but in the other direction, toward some trees by the edge of the meadow, then under a rock. Well, at least he was free now. I left the nest box on the rock pile and put one uneaten mouse on top of the box, in case Baby Weasel still needed a safe space and some ready food.

On each of the next five days, I left three small furry mice in the opening of the nest box to give Baby Weasel a "soft release" to the wild, in case he was having trouble hunting for his food. Each day the mice were gone and I replaced them with three more, as it seemed that Baby Weasel was still not hunting on his own and needed a supplement to his diet. On the sixth day, I noticed some raccoon scat on top of the nest box, proof a raccoon had been poaching some free mice meals! From then on, I left no more mice and hoped Baby Weasel was indeed surviving on his own.

Also at this time, between May and September when birds migrated to and from Vermont for the nesting season, I rehabbed and released three avian patients: a woodcock, a Cooper's hawk, and a merlin. The North American Woodcock, also known as the timberdoodle, is a squat wading bird with stubby legs, mottled light and dark brown plumage that helps camouflage it among the dead leaves on the forest floor, and a long bill, which it uses to probe the earth for earthworms and other insects. It came from Duxbury and had a wound on the top of its head where a cat had gotten it. It needed a dose of antibiotics to combat the bacteria in the cat's saliva, which would kill it if not treated within twenty-four hours. I gave it 0.2 cc of Baytril by mouth for seven days while I kept it in the Intensive Care Ward, where I made a nest of dry leaves. For its food, I put in a tub full of dirt with twelve night crawlers that the woodcock would eat as it probed the dirt. Eventually the woodcock was eating no less than thirty-six worms a day. I could tell she was probing the earth and getting the worms not only by the fact that the worms were gone, but also by the presence of dirt in her mouth when I pried open her long beak to give her antibiotic. In the early hours of the seventh day, May 25, around 5:30 A.M., I released the woodcock in the wet area across the road from our farmhouse after giving her a last dose of Baytril. She flapped her wings and walked into the underbrush, free once more.

My second patient, admitted at the end of August, was a Cooper's hawk that got hit by a car as it was eating a mouse in the road. It was in good flesh (incoming weight: 430 g., a female) and both wings were fine, but it had a swollen left eye and blood around its eye and beak. I gave it some Metacam, an anti-inflammatory steroid, and flushed the blood from around her eye using saline solution. By the third day, both eyes had swollen shut, the right eye evidently having a delayed reaction, and the hawk was effectively blind. I had to hand-feed her pieces of mouse every four hours. I also gave her eyedrops, which I was able to do by wrapping her in a "bird burrito," a towel wrapped over her wings, and prying open the lids. By evening, the right eyelid was already open again and the hawk was perching. When both eyes were open, the right eye was bright green while the left was its normal color, a pale yellow. After a couple of visits to the vet, it was determined that the hawk was blind in the right eye but still sighted in the left. Evidently, hemorrhaging in the right eye had mixed red blood with the yellow iris, making it show up green. Even though the initial impact seems to have been on the left side, a ricocheting concussive effect had done more damage on the right side. The vet said that, provided the hawk could eat on its own and pass a live prey test, I could still release her with one good eye.

When we got back from the vet, I immediately put the hawk out in the aviary, as I judged she had been cooped up in the cramped space of the Intensive Care Ward long enough. But would she eat on her own? For five days she didn't, and I had to catch her with the bird net once in the morning and once in the evening to feed her. I had a long talk with the vet and we agreed I might have to put the hawk down if her eye injury prevented her from focusing on prey. This would have been terribly disappointing, as I had been rehabbing this bird for three weeks now. But on the sixth day, lo and behold, the two mice I had put on the feeding platform two days ago were gone! Two days later, I conducted a live prey test with three live white mice I had bought at the pet store that I put into the garden pool. When I checked back a couple of hours later, two of the mice were gone and the third was looking rather cowed. I noticed blood on the shavings at the bottom of the pool and also some bird poop on the sill just above the mice. I released the hawk that weekend, in its home territory in Williamstown, where she flew off in a beautiful, ascending flight to a nearby tree.

Almost immediately when I got home from this release, I got a call about another bird, a merlin, who was found on the ground, stunned with one eye closed, on Stock Farm Road in Randolph. Merlins are small falcons, also known as "pigeon hawks" because their size resembles that of a pigeon, and they were used by noblewomen in the Middle Ages to practice falconry, as the birds were considered dainty enough to be suitable for the fairer sex. When the merlin was brought to me, she (as indicated by her brown plumage) was very feisty and, although thin, not starving. My guess was that she had been clipped by a car but was now recovering. I gave her some Metacam, fed her a pinkie mouse, and put her in the aviary. When I next tried to feed her, she flew round and round the aviary until she got tired and flew to the ground and I was able to net her. I fed her two pinkies and one small furry mouse. She clearly was in good flying shape and by the third day I decided to release her.

On the day of her release, in the morning, I managed to catch the merlin and fed her a last meal of two small furry mice. I released her back on Stock Farm Road in Randolph; the release site was a recently harvested cornfield backed by some woods that cradled a small pond on the edge of the field. Upon release from the carrier, the merlin flew to the right and far, far away to a distant tree, a beautiful flight. This was an easy win for the rehabber!

Otherwise, I faced long odds in treating avian patients. Over these five months, I took in a total of fifteen birds but was only able to release three, the rest having died or been euthanized. Five were struck by cars and had open-wound fractures to their wings, which could not be healed. Another five were so emaciated and starving that I could not save them, even by administering subQ fluids. Then there was a northern flicker (a woodpecker) that had flown into a house and died, and a great blue heron that was found in shallow water with an open-wound fracture on its leg, perhaps caused by a snapping turtle, and who had to be euthanized. Altogether, I had a recovery success rate during these five months of 20 percent, which I've been told is quite good for most efforts at wildlife rehabilitation. But nature can be cruel, and the damage caused by man is great, so it is hard to hope for anything better.

6

Second Winter

In October, as the weather turned colder, we decided to bring the beavers back inside for the winter. It was amazing how quickly we all reverted to our old routines. We were back to our daily chore of changing the water, both in the large and small tanks, and bringing down willow and poplar saplings for the beavers to chew on and cache under the ramp for winter. The beavers reverted to their favorite bedding spot by the furnace and their favorite sport, Beaver Wrestle, both inside and outside the water tanks. BK also reverted to his baby self, the one that liked to play or cuddle with us before he met Mrs. Beaver. When BK was swimming in the tank, Laura and I would get him to do his rolls and flips or push against us while clinging to our arms. Whenever Mrs. Beaver was preoccupied with swimming and not defending her man-territory, BK would cuddle with Laura. He would drape his whole body over Laura's lap and go limp. It was like having a living, breathing lap rug! Laura would scratch BK's side or rump, and he would nibble on her arm or finger, never biting too hard.

Even though the beavers were safely cached in the basement, we continued to be shadowed by the Department of Environmental Conservation and their enforcement action against us. For a while we thought we were off the hook, as it had been a couple weeks since we heard from the department. My last communication had been with the chief environmental enforcement officer, who I later learned was simply called "Chief" by his underlings. Chief called me on September 22, a week after one of his officers had paid us a visit. He reiterated that we had to take the enclosure out of the water, although he seemed open to compromise. For example, I proposed that I simply hoist the enclosure out of the water for half the year—during the winter and spring months, when the water was frozen or at high flow and I wouldn't be using it anyway—and then lower it back down into the water in summer and autumn, when it was rehabbing season. Chief said he would bring my proposal to the department for consideration. When I brought up the fact that my enclosure was not so different from underwater traps, which were also "solid discharges" and yet allowed in the water, Chief simply changed the subject.

Then, on October 8, I received a Notice of Alleged Violation (NOAV) from the DEC by certified mail. The letter, signed by Chief, officially informed me that I was in violation of Statute 1259a regarding "prohibited discharges" into state waters. My "alleged violation" was that I, the Respondent, had "placed a metal cage type structure into an unnamed tributary of Flint Brook" on our property. I was to "permanently remove" the said "cage structure" within fourteen days of receipt of the NOAV and inform the enforcement officer once the structure had been removed. The letter also threatened unspecified "penalties" as well as "corrective/restorative action" should I not comply. The letter spurred us to bring the beavers inside early in case the DEC came in with their enforcement officers and started dismantling the enclosure by force with the beavers still inside!

Three days later, Chief called me out of the blue, even though it was a state holiday, Indigenous Peoples' Day (formerly Columbus Day). I guess he was working overtime!

The first words out of Chief's mouth were that devices placed underwater to trap beavers had no relevance to my case, since trapping fell under the "separate statutory authority" of the Vermont Department of Fish and Wildlife (VDFW). I found this revealing. Here he was, on his day off work, calling me on a subject that he had refused to discuss in our first conversation back in September! This must've really worried him (or someone else higher up)!

In response, I brought up the fact that VDFW not only licensed trappers, but also licensed wildlife rehabbers, including letting us house patients in enclosures suitable to that species. I even quoted the relevant statutory authority: Title X Appendix, chapter 1, subchapter 9 of the Vermont Statutes!

"So you see," I said, "I am licensed to have this enclosure in the stream to rehab beavers, no less than trappers are licensed to put their traps in the water to trap them. If you prohibit my enclosure as a 'solid discharge,' then you must also declare all underwater trapping to be illegal!"

"W-w-well, I guess this will have to be decided by a judge," was all Chief could say. Our conversation quickly deteriorated after that. He was not willing to consider any compromise, such as keeping my enclosure for part of the year in the stream; my only option was to comply with the NOAV or face a fine. I said I would see him in court and hung up.

I was fuming. There is nothing quite so infuriating as fighting an implacable, immovable bureaucracy. I still did not know who had lodged this complaint against me in the first place. I was determined to find out.

With the help of POW and a lawyer with the Vermont Wildlife Coalition (VWC), I did. The lawyer wrote a "cease and desist" letter on my behalf, which stayed DEC's hand in enforcing their action against me for the time being. At the same time, he filed a Freedom of Information

Act (FOIA) request to see the full complaint record on my case. Even though the initial response was that this information was protected by "attorney-client privilege," six days later, a zip file suddenly appeared in my inbox containing DEC's entire correspondence relating to the complaint about my enclosure.

Boy, was this file revealing! A beaver trapper right here in town had filed the complaint. Beaver Killer, as I affectionately called him, was notorious for hating beavers and wanting to kill all the beavers in Roxbury. He once boasted that he had trapped 126 beavers in a season because, according to him, they were nothing more than "rats with tails." If he had his way, even orphaned kits would have to be euthanized, since without an enclosure, I wouldn't be able to rehab beavers. Beaver Killer learned of my enclosure after reading POW's Facebook post about moving back my enclosure after a storm, which he had then forwarded to the DEC.

But the case against me was weak. The file included the notes of a couple of water engineers at the DEC, who expressed doubts that their own department could really enforce Statute 1259a against my enclosure. They called it a "gray area," perhaps because the enclosure did not really obstruct water flow and was akin to underwater traps, which *were* legally allowed to be in the water. The engineers said, in the end, the department should instead rely on "other statutes if they want to chase this one." I also learned the enforcement officer who had visited our site had tried to enlist the aid of the local Fish and Wildlife game warden to accompany him. But the game warden refused, telling the officer that he had called his superiors, and they had told him "not to get involved" and "issue no directives." Why the VDFW did not want to touch my case was a mystery. Chief memoed the DEC commissioner, asking for his help in having a "conversation" with his counterpart at VDFW. Personally, I suspected the VDFW recognized that any rule enforcement against metal "cage-like" structures in the water would have jeopardized trapping of beavers, which they were determined to protect at all cost. Finally, internal memos indicated DEC higher-ups were very concerned about media coverage of the case, since my enclosure had already been featured in local newspapers.

It would be sweet revenge if Beaver Killer's complaint ended up backfiring against him, resulting in the end of his trapping of beavers. I considered filing a civil suit in Superior Court to try to compel the DEC to enforce Statute 1259a against the underwater trapping of beavers, but everyone told me I faced long odds in winning my case. As the VWC lawyer reminded me, the DEC undoubtedly has a cadre of high quality lawyers at their beck and call, and government agencies have broad, almost unlimited powers of enforcement that are difficult to contest in court. Nevertheless, I decided to file the suit anyway, because it's my firm belief that everyone should obey the law, trappers as well as rehabbers. As of this writing, the case is still pending; if, against the odds, I win, then it will be a great victory for the beavers.

In November, we found a way to comply with the NOAV. I managed to hoist the water side of the enclosure entirely out of the water so that there was no "discharge" as prohibited by Statute 1259a. The first time Laura and I tried to do this, though, it was a disaster. The two-by-four strapping attached to an overhanging pine tree that supported the hoist snapped in half as soon as it tried to bear the weight of the enclosure.

Two days later, we tried again. This time we used a much sturdier four-by-four post that was not only bolted to the pine tree but also propped underneath by an old aluminum extension ladder. By resting the bottom legs of the ladder on the bank, I was able to raise the beam bearing the hoist by gradually extending the ladder upward until the beam was in a horizontal position over the enclosure. The proof in the pudding was when I started pulling on the hoist chain: The enclosure shuddered and started rising, slowly, out of the water. The post groaned and bent slightly with the weight, but it held. Eventually I was able to lift the near-side of the enclosure about four to five feet above the water, while on the opposite bank, the chain-link fabric was just barely out of the water. It was like raising the drawbridge on a castle with the moat underneath!

Later that afternoon, the same DEC enforcement officer who had visited earlier just happened to stop by, unannounced. He congratulated us on being in "full compliance," took some photos, and left. We had hoisted the enclosure with only hours to spare!

It was not until two years later, long after the beavers had been released, that I fully dismantled the enclosure. I reused the dog kennel panels to enclose a small pond I had dug across from our old farmhouse, which was to serve as our new beaver rehab facility. The pond was fed by mountain runoff and had no direct connection to the stream. DEC need not interfere!

I got the idea for this new pond site from Pumpkin's mom. In mid-November, we went to see Miss Beaver at her new digs in southern Vermont. Her pond was about forty feet long and twenty feet wide, with a spring runoff feeding the pond on one side and flowing out through a man-made outlet on the other. The pond was enclosed by a wire fence about three feet high, with a wire "shelf" extending horizontally into the enclosure at the top and extending the same distance, about a foot, at the bottom on the ground. The great advantage of this site was that the beavers had full access to mud to play with, along with their sticks. Consequently, Miss Beaver and Pumpkin had built themselves a lodge out of mud, sticks, and leaves at the shallow end of the pond, where Pumpkin's mom had built a wire mesh cul-de-sac. The

LEFT: BK when he first arrived in early May 2020, at a week old. I put him in a baby sling as I worked on my laptop in the bathroom. BELOW: BK in his first "house," a hard plastic box tipped over on its side. He has a scrap of fur coat for warmth and a Beaver Buddy to keep him company.

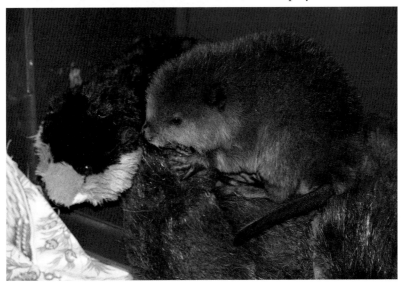

ABOVE: Laura feeding BK, without having to use her hands. BK fed himself by sucking on the cannula-tipped syringe while holding it in his paws. LEFT: BK swimming in the outdoor pool. He took to the water right away, without me having to help him in any way.

ABOVE: BK in the outdoor pool, showing off his flipper feet. Beavers are remarkably well-adapted for aquatic environments, such as having hind feet with webbing in between their toes. RIGHT: BK in his wooden house, scratching himself under the chin and showing off his incisors. A beaver's incisors are orange due to the iron in the teeth that keeps them strong.

RIGHT: BK giving a great yawn. He typically yawned after an exercise session, waddling and galumphing over the lawn. BELOW: BK on the edge of the lawn, standing up, alert. He seems to be listening to something, perhaps the sound of the gurgling stream that was not fifty feet behind him, in the woods.

ABOVE: BK sleeping in the crook of my arm. What dreams do beavers dream?
BELOW: BK just after he had a swim in the outdoor pool, reaching for my hand with his paw. For me, this symbolizes how we can forge a connection with a wild animal across the species divide. However, beavers are uniquely social animals, which makes their rehab different from that of other species.

RIGHT: Long-eared owl, as a nestling, when she first arrived two days after BK. Her yellow eyes and little fuzzy horns starting on the top of her head distinguish her from our most common owl, the barred owl.
BELOW: Long-eared owl, just twenty days later, in her adult plumage. Long-eared owls are distinguished by their prominent ear tufts and streaked or mottled plumage, which provides excellent camouflage in forested areas.

ABOVE: BK training to use a ramp to get in and out of his outdoor pool. The rope on the rope swing board helped give him traction for getting in and out of the water, although he was often more interested in simply chewing on it! BELOW: BK in his Dogloo in the outdoor enclosure. He was especially comfortable lying in his flamingo-themed dogbed with a stick to chew on!

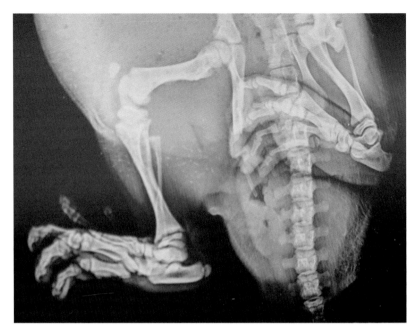

ABOVE: An x-ray of BK's abdomen when he was almost three months old. The os penis can be seen just to the left of the spine and underneath the third toe of his left hind foot, which he is holding up higher than his right. BELOW: BK taking a break from swimming in the Auld Cove, reaching up to sniff and hold my hand. I'm sitting on a log that conveniently stretches out across the cove.

RIGHT: BK swimming in his Swimway, a ten by thirty foot stretch of water just upstream from the Auld Cove. BK liked to swim laps here as Laura and I watched from folding chairs set up on the grassy sward on the Swimway's eastern bank. BELOW: BK chewing on my shoelaces. He also enjoyed wrestling with the towel in the lower right-hand corner of the photo.

RIGHT: Carrying BK back to his enclosure from the stream. This was always a very wet experience! BELOW: BK swimming in the Auld Cove in autumn. At this time of year, a carpet of leaves was always falling onto the flowing surface of the water, which BK had to swim through.

LEFT: Mr. Chipmunk, who began stealing BK's Rodent Chow nuggets from the outdoor enclosure in August. Mr. Chipmunk outwitted all my anti-theft efforts until I hit upon the solution of only giving BK nuggets when he was in the enclosure and putting them in the Dogloo, where he could guard them. BELOW: BK and Big Teddy Bear in the basement. Orphaned beaver kits must spend at least their first winter indoors. Otherwise, they risk freezing to death out in the lodge, even with other kits for company, because there is not enough body mass for them to keep warm and survive in northern climes.

Me grooming BK, and BK grooming me back. Although BK used his incisors on my skin, he recognized that it was not the same as beaver hide and was always very gentle, giving me "love nibbles" as I itched his flank. During the long winter months, beaver families undoubtedly spend hours grooming each other in such a fashion in the lodge.

A female snowy owl, whom I tried to rescue in December 2020. The owl had wandered into a cow barn in Irasburg, weak and starving. Whenever there is an "irruption," or large brood production, of any species in a given year, they often compete for food resources, and inevitably some do not feed well enough to survive.

Laura with Pumpkin, another orphaned beaver kit raised by a rehabber, in southern Vermont, who we took in during the month of January and hoped would be a mate for BK. Unfortunately, "she" turned out to be a he, and two beavers of the same sex from different colonies cannot coexist in the same territory.

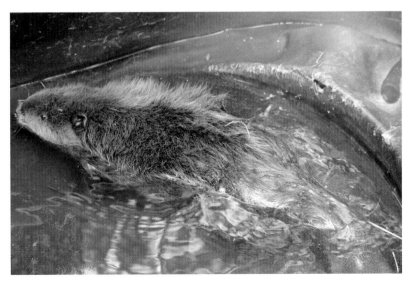

Miss Beaver swimming in the outdoor pool. She was a two-year-old that had dispersed from her colony and was attacked by a dog and found in the backyard of a house on Main Street in Stowe. After treating her wounds for two months, we mated her with Pumpkin and she became a mother and grandmother.

Mrs. Beaver, who came to us in May 2021 and won the Mating Game, bonding with BK. She was also a yearling orphaned beaver, from Benson, VT, but fifteen pounds lighter than BK. We could also tell her apart from BK by her darker, brown fur and her prominent, "bug" eyes.

BK (on left) and Mrs. Beaver snuggling. After nearly a month-long "courtship," in which the two beavers occupied separate spaces in our basement enclosure, I came down one morning to find the two sleeping on the same pad. Somehow, they had figured out how to be together in spite of a metal railing dividing them.

ABOVE: The new outdoor enclosure where I housed the beavers from July to October 2021. Comprised of dog kennel panels and chain-link fabric on both the top and bottom, the enclosure allowed the beavers to swim in the stream whenever they wanted. Eventually, I replaced this enclosure with one encompassing a small, man-made pond. BELOW: The release house, set up at an abandoned beaver pond in Woodbury, VT. We released the beavers in May 2022, on land owned by the Northeast Wilderness Trust (NEWT). The house provides beavers with a safe space while they acclimatize to their release site. A kind of "covered bridge" gives them direct access from the house to the water.

My last glimpse of BK, as he was swimming in the pond, on July 5, 2022. Laura and I were carrying away the remnants of the release house when she took this photo.

lodge was built against one side of the mesh so you could see into it as the beavers lay side by side in a "69" position. It made for fascinating viewing, but in the winter, Pumpkin's mom would have to put a piece of foam insulation against the wire mesh to fully insulate the lodge. In my old enclosure, with the chain-link fabric covering the ground, and therefore the mud, the beavers had no opportunity to learn this skill.

As we muddled through the long winter months, I occupied myself with saving a couple of barred owls from starvation. Every winter, there are some owls who have a hard time hunting and therefore fall behind in their feeding. To bring them back to the land of the living, I not only have to get them eating solid food again, but also get their wing strength back after muscles atrophied during starvation. I do this by conducting some physical therapy sessions—namely, by having the owls fly back and forth, back and forth, across the aviary. This was so successful that I was able to release one owl in Waitsfield after a month of rehab and another, from Colchester, in just two weeks.

Meanwhile, the beavers were going a little stir-crazy down in the basement. There were numerous signs, most of which had to do with Mrs. Beaver, who perhaps felt less at home in our basement than BK. For one thing, when I came downstairs, I would sometimes be greeted by Mrs. Beaver almost at eye level, face to face. She achieved this by perching on the lip of the large tank at the deep end like some large, furry owl. She would be facing toward the railing and the stairs, leaning precariously over the concrete abyss two feet below, with her paws resting on the railing itself. She appeared to be looking for a way to leap out of the enclosure without hurting herself. I would gently nudge her back into the tank, into which she dived like a cannonball, making a great splash! But one day I found Mrs. Beaver perching on the tank lip at the other shallow end, with her back to me, facing the concrete wall. There was no danger of her falling over the railing at this corner, because right next to the railing was our basement wall, blocking any further advance. But this did not stop Mrs. Beaver! When I got closer, I saw Mrs. Beaver was busy chewing on the concrete! It was as if she was trying to chew her way out of the basement. After I shooed her back into the water, I could see her teeth marks on the concrete wall, forever marking her presence.

The wall was not the only thing Mrs. Beaver would chew on. She was also chewing on the coated wire protecting the underside of the basement stairs, perhaps hoping to find a way out that way. I came down one day to find a section of the wire chewed right off, lying on the ground inside the enclosure. I was afraid the beavers might hurt themselves on one of the sharp ends of the wire. BK, for example, got a mouth infection last September that necessitated taking him to the vet for a shot of Convenia antibiotic; it may have been from chewing on wire that poked his mouth. Now, Mrs. Beaver was chewing the wire, and I didn't know how to make her stop. I thought I found a solution in the form of the wood swing seat that had two drilled holes at either end, which we had used to make a ramp for BK and then for Miss Beaver when they were in the outdoor enclosure. I threaded bailing twine through the holes and attached the board to the wire so it served as a sacrificial shield Mrs. Beaver could chew instead of the wire. As Laura and I were doing this, BK came to check out what we were doing while Mrs. Beaver stayed in bed. By the time I came down later to change the beavers' water, either BK or Mrs. Beaver had chewed through the top bailing twine, so the board was flat on the floor. I then watched as Mrs. Beaver did a big pee right over the board, forming a great puddle of opaque liquid. I quickly got a towel and mopped up the pee, but then BK came over and also peed in a great streak near the same spot! Laura suggested they were marking their territory, because the board smelled like another beaver—namely, Miss Beaver. Now, instead of the board distracting them from the wire spot, the beavers became obsessed with the board itself. To distract them, Laura cleaned out all the sticks and other woody detritus from underneath the ramp and by the large tank and moved them to the other side of the enclosure. This upset the beavers, who immediately commenced moving all the sticks back, a task that occupied them for the rest of the day.

The last thing Mrs. Beaver did that winter that drove me crazy was to pull out the garden hose from the large tank as I was attempting to fill it, causing water to start flooding the basement. I interpreted this as a teenager's rebellion along the lines of, "Well, if you're not going to bring me back out into the stream, I'm going to bring the stream into the basement!" Mrs. Beaver was deliberately trying to flood the basement, perhaps to turn it into her own private indoor pond! Usually if I changed the water in the morning, there was no problem, as the beavers were still in bed and I could drain and fill the large tank undisturbed. But if I was late and let the morning get away from me, I was in trouble. If I was upstairs while the tank was filling, I invariably heard an ominous "thump" downstairs. I would come down to find the hose out of the tank and Mrs. Beaver with a guilty look on her face. One day Mrs. Beaver succeeded to the point that she was able to drink from a pool of water on the floor by the deep end of the large tank! I had to dry all the rubber stall mats at that end before mold grew on their undersides, and I had to pull up all the sopping wet bedding and blankets the beavers slept on by the furnace.

A related danger was that Mrs. Beaver would chew on the electrical cord of the sump pump as it was draining the tank. This ran the risk, of course, of Mrs. Beaver inadvertently electrocuting herself. One time I pulled the cord from Mrs. Beaver's mouth just as she was beginning to chew and break through the plastic casing to expose the live wire underneath. She was OK, but it was a close call. A second time, I came down in the afternoon to find the cord of the sump pump severed, even though it had been stored away and was not in use. While the pump itself was stored some distance from the enclosure, its cord was lying near enough that one of the beavers was able to reach through the bars of the railing and pull it through. I was really annoyed at those naughty beavers! Laura's brother, an amateur electrician, promised he could splice the cord back together when he came over that weekend. In the meantime, we had a spare pump stored in our tack room, which I commandeered the next morning to change the beavers' water. It worked so well that I was able to drain the large tank in about half the time. This was because the pump's suction holes were on the side rim of the bottom pad, instead of on the very bottom; this way, they were far less likely to get plugged up with beaver gunk. Maybe the beavers knew what they were doing after all!

Even though BK could generally be absolved of this stir-craziness, he was not entirely blameless. He loved to push on the metal railing, especially in the evening as we were trying to go to sleep, making that horrible scraping sound across the concrete floor that sounded like nails on a chalkboard. Sometimes I think Mrs. Beaver joined in on this activity judging from the staccato rhythms!

But in other ways, the beavers seemed to be enjoying their time indoors, insulated from the cold weather. They could do things down in the basement, such as Beaver Wrestle, that they couldn't do in the cramped space of a lodge. They also had fresh water every day, freely available simply by walking up the ramp and diving into the tank, instead of braving ice-cold water underneath a blanket of ice and snow. Mrs. Beaver, as usual, got into the large tank as soon as she could, right after I drained and cleaned it and starting filling it with water. One time, as I was taking out the hose while Mrs. Beaver was swimming around a full tank, some water happened to drip from the hose right onto Mrs. Beaver's back. She didn't like that and let her feelings be known by doing a tumble turn and slapping the water hard with her tail, making a big splash that drenched me!

Another advantage the beavers had over their wild cousins was they always had warm, dry furry pads fresh from the dryer to sleep on, and room to stretch as they slept. Mrs. Beaver, in particular, enjoyed this in extravagantly decadent fashion, lying flat on her back, her belly exposed, her paws and hind feet hanging loose in the air, and her mouth lolling open, showing her teeth. Clearly Mrs. Beaver felt safe and relaxed in her basement home, even if she'd rather be outside. The beavers also greatly enjoyed regular access to Rodent Chow nuggets, as well as the occasional apple or carrot treat, which they typically begged for at the railing just in front of the Vittles Vault that contained the nuggets. Laura wondered how they'd survive in the wild without these supplements to their diet. I tried to reassure her they'd find tasty substitutes, such as water lilies or pondweed, or even apples growing close to the pond or riverbank where they'd be released.

Our beavers were so well nourished on willow sticks and nuggets that they were quickly gaining weight. We weighed both of them in early January: BK weighed in at forty-four pounds without the tail, forty-five pounds with the tail. Mrs. Beaver came in at forty-two pounds without the tail, forty-three pounds with the tail. He had gained about seven pounds since we last weighed him back in August, and she had gained ten pounds!

The beavers were remarkably affectionate toward each other, grooming each other as they lay side by side in bed. If they were lying nose to nose, BK might scratch Mrs. Beaver under her chin using his forepaws or nibble on her neck, while she might gently nibble on BK's face or on his belly. If they were lying head to tail, then they would nibble on each other's rear ends. The value of these grooming sessions to Mrs. Beaver was illustrated by the fact that she drove Laura off whenever Laura tried to groom BK herself. If left to their own devices, on the other hand, there was the danger that the beaver wouldn't finish the grooming job. One time as I was changing the water in the large tank, I watched Mrs. Beaver sitting on her tail next to BK, trying to groom her belly. But then she began bending over farther and farther, until it became clear that she'd fallen asleep! Suddenly she woke and resumed grooming herself, but she soon gave that up to go to bed properly, resting her head on BK's flank and using it as her pillow.

When one beaver yawned, the other yawned. If one was having a spa soak in the small tank, the other, often as not, was floating alongside so they barely fit in the tank, the water displaced to the very lip of the rim. Even when playing Beaver Wrestle, they were gentle in that when they locked faces, they never once used their teeth on each other, but instead used their forepaws as leverage, grabbing hold of a fold in the other's fur as they pushed off their hind legs. All this made me think how sad it would be if, once they were released, one or the other was caught by a trapper, leaving the other bereft and alone in this world.

But as March arrived, we all began to sniff spring in the air, and I knew we would have to start thinking about releasing the beavers, this time for good. We were entering the final chapter of their time with us, the last leg of a long journey. It was a bittersweet time: I felt sad and glad, relieved but also fearful.

7

Back to the Wild

L ooking for that special place to release your beaver? Look no further than Woodbury Mountain, located in beautiful Woodbury, VT! We are a highly selective Nature Reserve, administered by the Northeast Wilderness Trust. We are very remote, accessible only by a fourth-class road, where absolutely no trapping is allowed! Our community of beavers is very respectful of other beavers' territory, while at the same time happy to abandon sites so new beavers can move in! Each pond comes with its own dam and lodge just begging to be maintained by new occupants! Act now before another beaver takes your beaver's place!

I still remember the stressful ordeal of applying to colleges in my senior year of high school: leafing through prospectuses, visiting campuses, filling out applications, waiting for the letters of admission or rejection to come in the mail.

I experienced all those feelings again, this time as the parent of a beaver-child. Laura and I were searching high and low to find BK and his girlfriend just the right place where they could swim, chew trees, and build dams and lodges while remaining unmolested by rival beavers looking to muscle in on their territory. It was hard to find. Any site promising for beaver occupation was as likely as not to be already occupied by other beavers. Once there was an active beaver pond, one had to give it at least a mile-long berth upstream and downstream, because beavers are territorial and will march that far to extirpate rival colonies. Finding a suitable release site was the hardest part of beaver rehab.

Our first-choice release site for our beavers was right here on our own property, just upstream from where we had the outdoor enclosure. For many, local is less than desirable when choosing the college experience of finally being launched out into the world. But for Laura and me, it was ideal. We could keep an eye on BK and Mrs. Beaver, protect them, and make sure they'd want for nothing as they made their start in life. Admittedly, this might be considered helicopter beaver parenting—as if human parents went away to college *with* their child—but BK was our firstborn, so to speak, and we didn't want anything to happen to him.

The site I had in mind was dredged from my childhood memories of a beaver pond just down the bank from a meadow across from our old farmhouse. It was said that some teenage boys shot the beavers living there before my family bought the farm in '67, but I remember the beavers coming back for a little while, complete with a dam and a lodge, in the seventies. But then there were no more beavers, and the whole site was overgrown with thick, woody shrubs and thickets. Laura and I thought if we built a Beaver Dam Analog (BDA) on the stream, the site would start flooding again and our beavers could finish the job. BDAs are simple wooden structures, such as a wall of planks attached to posts sunk into stream beds, and are often used on sites where owners want to reintroduce beavers and give them a head start, incentivizing them to stay. Beaver Lady advised me that our release would be far more successful if the beavers were released into a pond rather than a running stream. The trouble was, we had no idea about how to build a BDA.

That's when we turned to Skip Lisle, Mr. Beaver Deceiver. Mr. Beaver Deceiver (aka The Castor Master) was the famed inventor of the Beaver Baffle, although he prefers the term Flow Device. Flow Devices are basically wire cages or "filters" typically installed at the openings of road culverts to both protect them from being dammed by beavers and slow water flow so beavers are "deceived" into thinking that they don't need to dam the culvert.* The overall goal, of course, is that town road crews and transportation authorities don't have to resort to trapping and killing the beavers. Like Beaver Lady, Mr. Beaver Deceiver had over thirty years of experience in his beaver-related field of expertise. He had built a wire fence for Pumpkin's mom so she could enclose the pond where Pumpkin and Miss Beaver had spent the winter and were now raising a litter of kits. (Henceforth, Miss Beaver was to be known as Mother Beaver!**) He agreed to help us as well.

To prepare for Mr. Beaver Deceiver's visit on the twentieth of April, Laura and I spent a whole day dismantling an unused horse fence in the meadow just above the stream where we'd put the BDA, or what Mr. Beaver Deceiver preferred to call a "starter dam." We made a great pile of

---

* As Mr. Beaver Deceiver would be first to point out, however, Flow Devices vary considerably depending on the demands of the topography of the site. These days, Mr. Beaver Deceiver builds a much more sophisticated engineered device than a simple "exclusion fence." In addition to a square fence "filter" installed directly around the culvert opening, Mr. Beaver Deceiver also installs a pipe going from inside the square fence filter farther into the pond, where there is an additional square "filter" protecting the intake end. This does two things: It more effectively "sneaks" water away from the culvert so beavers' damming instinct is less likely to be triggered; and it allows for water flow through the culvert even if the filter around the culvert opening is dammed.

** As of this writing, one of Miss Beaver's kits has now had kits, making her Grandmother Beaver!

old hemlock boards to use in the BDA. I also went to the lumber supply store and got some two-by-threes to use as posts that we would drive into the stream bed.

On the appointed day, Mr. Beaver Deceiver arrived to inspect our site. His assessment was, unfortunately, that the BDA wouldn't work. He said that, because of the topography of the site, the BDA would have to extend a long way beyond the immediate bank of the stream, and the water flow of the stream was too high at the moment to be able to dam it effectively and create a usable pond. There was also not enough food for the beavers at this site, since most of the trees were softwoods or pine trees, which beavers wouldn't eat. They also overshadowed everything and prevented good food like aspen from growing.

We were not releasing the beavers here. In truth, it was a bitter blow. The next day, Laura and I came down in the evening to check on the beavers. Laura got into the enclosure and cuddled with BK; it was her way of saying goodbye, that we'd miss him when we released him, now that we were going to have to release him farther away. She came down later and did this a second time that night.

We still had a couple of fallback sites. Our second potential release site was also in Roxbury, just up the road about a mile from our place, where we could at least keep an occasional eye on the beavers. It was owned by an eighty-nine-year-old old-timer I'll call Lazarus, who didn't know if he'd make it through another Vermont winter and was thinking of moving down to Texas to be with his daughter. He wouldn't be selling his property right away and was open to letting me release the beavers there. It was a beautiful site, with two big ponds hemmed in by two large dams and a beaver lodge in the lower pond. I didn't see any evidence of beaver activity, only a lot of old chewed stumps, but it was hard to be sure. Laura and I returned at dusk, around 7:00 P.M., to check if there was any beaver activity. We hiked through the marsh right up to the lodge. Two geese began making a racket in the pond, disturbed that we were there. Peepers were making a racket all around us, and a hawk was watching from a nearby dead tree. We saw no beavers, but on the way out I saw the stump of what looked like a freshly chewed tree. Even so, there was very little food here, which may have been why beavers had left, if that is, in fact, what they had done. Laura was not impressed and didn't think it was the right site.

We were left with our second fallback and third potential release site in Monkton. It was owned by a man I'll call Mr. Magoo, who took me on a tour of the site a couple of years ago. Back then, the resident beavers had been eaten by some coyotes, so there were predators. But it was a big, beautiful pond, with an existing dam and lodges. Now, two years on, Mr. Magoo said he checked the dam and saw that something had repaired it, moving mud around, so it seemed beavers were back. He emailed me some pictures, and I could see paw prints in the mud as well as a recently chewed stick. We couldn't release the beavers at Monkton either.

I was now all out of fallbacks, and it was back to square one as far as finding a release site for the beavers. I was beginning to enter panic mode. It was the beginning of May, and I should have been preparing the beavers for their return to the wild. BK and Mrs. Beaver seemed to sense my anxiety, as they started to take down the ramp leading to the big tank for several nights in a row. It was as if they were protesting having to be restricted to such a small water space when they should be splashing around in a big pond! Their natural instinct may also have been kicking in, as young beavers in the wild typically disperse and strike out on their own soon after their second year to form their own colonies. I wanted to release the beavers soon to give them plenty of time in the summer and fall to construct their own dams and lodges and settle into their new home before winter. I was determined to give them as much of a head start as possible.

At least the beavers had bulked up over the winter. We weighed them both on May 5, and each came in at fifty pounds! This was toward the upper limit of the weight range of mature two- or three-year-old beavers, which was between thirty and sixty pounds. They were full adults now and had enough fat reserves that I felt confident they could survive their next winter.

Then a miracle happened. I got a lead on a potential release site for the beavers! Protect Our Wildlife put me in touch with the Northeast Wilderness Trust (NEWT), which owned six thousand acres in Woodbury, VT. The NEWT president welcomed the release of my beavers in the Woodbury Mountain Wilderness Preserve, but she cautioned that much of it was already occupied. I resolved to check a couple promising sites that weekend, the second Sunday of the month.

One site was called Mud Pond, located in the northern part of the preserve, near where Woodbury met the adjacent town of Hardwick just south of Buffalo Mountain Road. We drove up Route 14 through East Montpelier, then Woodbury, and finally came to the town line of Hardwick, where we found the address that seemed to be the property closest to Mud Pond. But then we saw a big Trump flag hanging from the house porch and decided this would not be the best place at which to stop. We went to the next driveway, which winded up a hill. A sign said, "Moose Crossing," which I took as a good sign, and we continued up the driveway to a rustic log cabin at the top of the rise. I got out and knocked, but it appeared that no one was home until a yellow lab came bounding around the corner of the house. He was friendly enough, wagging his tail, so I petted him and called out. I was answered by an old gentleman, perhaps in his seventies, who looked like the quintessential grizzled Old Vermonter with his red suspenders.

I explained that I was a wildlife rehabilitator looking at Mud Pond as a potential release site for two beavers I had been rehabbing for the past two years. Old Vermonter called to his dog, Moose, which would explain the "Moose Crossing" sign. He said he knew everything there was to know in this town—he was on the Planning Commission and had been for years—so he reckoned he could help. He invited me into his house. Moose and I entered through the door Old Vermonter held open for us. The house was simple, with an open floor plan, the kitchen, dining, and living rooms all occupying a single space. On the table was a number of rolled maps, which looked like official town maps you'd use in a Planning Commission. If there was a lot of clutter, it was tidy clutter: a typical bachelor pad, judging from the complete lack of any feminine presence. If Old Vermonter had once been married, he was not now.

Old Vermonter began unrolling and examining his maps, but none appeared to have roads on them. He then remembered he had a Vermont Gazetteer, which looked to be new. He pointed out Buffalo Mountain Road and told me to take that road until my car couldn't go any farther, which was after I had passed the last house and a sugar shack. Then I should walk to where a stream that fed Mud Pond crossed the road and follow the stream to the pond itself. But he warned there were at least three beaver ponds between Buffalo Mountain Road and Mud Pond. Old Vermonter complained, "Those beavers are having so many babies, they're taking over and colonizing all the streams and ponds over there." It looked like I couldn't release my beavers in Mud Pond.

I asked about another potential release site, this one farther south, off Woodbury Mountain Road. Old Vermonter didn't know anything about that country, but he told me how to get there. "Take a right out of here and go up to the rise where there is a four-corner intersection. There'll be a gravel road on your right and a gravel road on your left. Take the right. That's what we call the County Road. Follow that down, and Woodbury Mountain Road will be on your right." I thanked him and shook his hand.

We found the County Road and followed it a long way south, until we came to a hand-painted sign that said, "Woodbury Mountain Road." The sign had some funky colored decorations with a directional pointer underneath. Judging from the sign, the road was bound to be less than ordinary, and this proved to be the case. It was a rough road. At several places large gravel rocks had been dumped just to make it passable. Many rocks looked sharp and pointy, and we were deathly afraid we were going to pop a tire. Eventually we stopped the car and I set out to walk the rest of the way on foot, leaving Laura in the car on the very slim chance that another vehicle came along.

I passed a log landing with many logs piled on both sides of the road and a log loader parked off to the side. I walked on, up hill after hill, and I had to stop several times to catch my breath. A stream meandered from one side of the road to the other; eventually it migrated under a culvert back to the left side, where I knew the pond was. After about half a mile, I came to what looked like a sandy pull-off on the left side of the road and knew I was close. I recognized it from Google Earth as being just south of the pond. After ascending the rise, I caught a glimpse of the pond on my left. I walked through the trees until I found the grassy remains of an old logging road leading to the pond. The pond was at least two acres, with an old beaver dam enclosing it on its southern edge. At the northern end of the pond, some young woody saplings were growing that looked like good beaver food. I found an old, weathered stick chewed by a beaver, but nothing recent.

This seemed as good a place as any for a release: remote, isolated, reachable by road but one little traveled, a large pond with plenty of woody growth on its perimeter, and an already-constructed beaver dam with no evidence of other beavers on-site! When we got back home, I went downstairs to give the beavers the good news. BK came running over, but all he wanted was nuggets, and soon he was joined at the railing by Mrs. Beaver, who begged also. I obliged, filling each of their metal dishes. What would they do in the wild without their nuggets?

Now that I had a release site, I spent the next week and a half constructing a release house that would temporarily house the beavers until they built their own lodge. Beaver

Lady e-mailed me the plans. The house was quite simple: a plywood box measuring four-by-three feet and thirty-two inches high. I also constructed a ramp that was six feet long and enclosed on all sides, so the beavers could get in and out of the water from their house without encountering any predators—like a miniature covered bridge.

The day before the release, we tested the release house in the outdoor enclosure. We needed to know if BK and Mrs. Beaver would be OK with using it as their new home in the wild. With the release house assembled inside the enclosure, together with the covered bridge ramp going from the house to the water, I hoisted the enclosure back into the stream, like lowering the drawbridge on a castle. We carried BK out first, as he was happy to just wander into the carrier to go on another adventure. Laura and I had to put him on a hand truck and wheel him down to the water, he was now so heavy! We lifted the carrier into the release house and opened the carrier door. BK immediately came out and went down the ramp and out into the water, where he swam around on both sides of the ramp. He then went back up the ramp into the house and back down again. BK was so smart and so brave! What release site wouldn't want him?

We then did the same with Mrs. Beaver. She was just as heavy as BK, if not heavier. Mrs. Beaver was a little more hesitant to go down the ramp, and it was only when BK came up the ramp and into the house that she was persuaded to follow, after a quick bout of Beaver Wrestle inside the house. She was happy to swim around with BK, and they wrestled a couple more times in the water. Then it was Mrs. Beaver's turn to come back up the ramp into the house, twice! Laura and I were so proud, and so relieved.

We rewarded the beavers with some fresh-cut willow sticks. BK came out of the water and waddled over to us, where we fussed over and petted him, before he went back into the water. We watched them for a bit and then went inside when it started to rain. After my afternoon bus run, I went and checked on the beavers from the top of the bank looking down on the enclosure. I could barely see the shadow of a beaver in the entrance of the ramp. Evidently they had scurried back into the ramp and release house, now their safe space, when hearing a stranger approach. Eventually BK came out and swam around, while Mrs. Beaver watched from just inside the covered ramp. When I came down the bank to get a closer look, BK scurried back into the ramp. Later, Laura and I came out to the enclosure to give them nuggets and a blanket. We lifted the lid to find both beavers in the house. BK had brought a bunch of wet leaves and sticks into the house and ramp. Laura filled two metal dishes and put them on the floor of the house and also put the blanket on top of the horse pad. Both beavers then ran out of the house and down the ramp into the water. Laura remarked that BK seemed especially happy with the house.

On May 20, the day of their release, Laura and I checked on the beavers in the morning, and they were both sleeping in their new house. Around 1:00 P.M. I began dismantling their house, now that they were both up. BK looked forlorn as I took his walls away, one by one. But soon he and Mrs. Beaver contented themselves with swimming in the stream. I carried each plywood panel to the truck. Flower Girl and her family arrived around 1:45 P.M. and helped us load the covered ramp and all the willow that we were to leave with them at their release site, which included some fresh-cut willow Flower Girl had brought.

We were now ready to bring out the beavers. I brought in the carrier and Laura called BK in from the stream; he obligingly came waddling up and went right into the carrier. We carried him to the car and put him in the metal dog crate set up in the back. We then had to get Mrs. Beaver in the carrier, which proved harder. She was out in the stream, swimming around and chewing on sticks, and generally refusing to come in. Eventually Laura came into the enclosure just to lure Mrs. Beaver out because she always hated Laura and wanted to drive her out of the enclosure! When she came up out of the water I was able to manhandle her, with much complaining, into the carrier, pushing her big butt in. Flower Girl and her husband carried her back to the car, where we put her in the back, facing BK. We were ready to head out.

It took us an hour to travel on Route 12 to Montpelier and then on the County Road to Calais and Woodbury before turning onto the Woodbury Mountain Road. There was no sign of the NEWT people, so I left Laura and the beavers to wait for them while I took the truck to the site. As I was bringing willow sticks down to the pond, the NEWT people finally showed and helped me bring down the rest of the willow, the covered ramp, and the panels of the release house. I put the house together with help from one of the NEWTs. All the while, ferocious black-flies were making a meal of me. I finally got the house together at the edge of the pond and attached the covered ramp, with one end in a deep pool of water. We were ready to bring down the beavers!

With the NEWT people piled in the truck bed, we made our way to where Laura was parked. We loaded the beavers into the bed: first Mrs. Beaver in the carrier, then BK in the dog crate, facing each other once again. BK had peed and soiled himself, making a slurry mess in the bottom tray of the crate. Clearly he was stressed, but his ordeal was almost over. The NEWT people climbed into the truck bed, carefully positioning themselves around the beavers, and Laura sat next to me in the cab. We traveled slowly and bumpily to the release site. I and the NEWT director (she had traveled in her own SUV) carried BK down in the crate, while two other NEWTs carried Mrs. Beaver. Once I had to stop to wipe away a blackfly that was chowing down on my right eye. When we reached the release house by the water's edge, I covered the ramp hole inside the house with a piece of plywood and we put Mrs. Beaver in the house first. Then we loaded BK into the carrier and put him in the house, making sure not to squash Mrs. Beaver. We closed the lid and let them be for a bit, hoping they'd settle. Laura and the NEWT director took up positions on the old beaver dam to film the release. After a short while, the beavers figured out how to move the plywood panel aside and went down the ramp into the water. They had released themselves!

Both beavers began swimming around, exploring their new surroundings. BK did some dives and somersaults in the water while Mrs. Beaver explored the willow we had put into the shallows by the release house. We also dumped a bag of carrots and a whole big bag of Mazuri nuggets into the house as their food stash. Then BK started coming out of the water and waddling up the path toward the road! Did he want to go home with us? Laura had to head him off and lead him back down to the water, telling him this was his new home. Soon we lost sight of him as he swam around a corner of the dam. Mrs. Beaver, on the other hand, stayed close by the house and started coming out of the water toward the NEWTs, presumably to push them out of her new territory. It was time to leave. I gathered my drill and screws and the NEWTS carried the carrier and the dog crate and we headed back up the path to the road. I couldn't see BK, but Mrs. Beaver was still swimming around the house. When I was back in the truck, I looked in the mirror and saw my right eye was puffy and almost closed, while both arms and legs were covered with bloody blackfly bites, as if I had a case of smallpox. These were my scars from the beaver release, but I was happy to bear them.

Like all goodbyes, our farewell to the beavers was an emotional rollercoaster. On the one hand, I was happy to see them back in the wild where they belonged, and I was relieved that we were no longer responsible for them. They were healthy and able to be independent. On the other hand, I was sad to see them go and no longer have them as part of our lives. For two years, they were part of our family. I had grown used to having them around. I would truly miss BK Time, Cuddles, and Beaver Wrestle. After all, it was not everyone who could say they had beavers in the basement!

Some things I was *not* going to miss included changing the beavers' water and hearing the ear-splitting scraping sounds as they pushed the metal railing across the concrete floor. The day after the release, a Saturday, I drained the large and small tanks for the last time, then rinsed them and threw out the poo water. It brought home to me that the beavers were really and truly gone. BK was on his own. I thought of the family he and Mrs. Beaver might one day raise.

Four days after the release, we decided to go back
to Woodbury Mountain Road to check on the beavers.
On the way we stopped to get some carrots and apples.
When we got there, we walked down to the pond but
could see no beavers. I unscrewed the lid on the release
house and opened it up, but no beavers. Just a whole lot of
crushed nuggets that looked soggy, as if they had been
flattened by wet beavers. Then Laura began calling for BK
while she walked west along the top of the dam. I walked
north along the water's edge, but could see no evidence of
a lodge being built on the opposite bank. I began following
Laura along the top of the dam. Did the beavers abandon
the site? Suddenly, Laura called to me, saying BK was
swimming my way. Then I saw him. He was moving fast
through the water, like a torpedo, his nose and the upper
part of his body just barely skimming the surface. Laura
threw an apple into the water, and I cut an apple in my
hand in half to offer to him. But he wasn't interested in
the apple. He was only interested in this intruder into his
territory. BK came onto the bank of the dam and hissed
at me repeatedly. It was as if he didn't know who I was!
I scratched him on the top of his head but didn't dare
do more.

Meanwhile, Mrs. Beaver was also swimming our way,
but underwater; I could barely make out her distorted form
just below the surface. She joined BK on the dam and I
started to panic. I didn't know if I could fend off *two* angry

beavers! Laura arrived with a stick, prepared to protect me from Mrs. Beaver. Suddenly, BK and Mrs. Beaver started wrestling with each other. Were they trying to blow off some of their aggressiveness? We made our way back along the dam to the release house, put the apple halves and carrots in the house, closed the lid, and I hurriedly screwed the top back on. BK started swimming over to us again, and we beat a hasty retreat.

Back in the car, we told ourselves that we were happy. The beavers had stayed together at the pond site. They seemed to have settled in and established their territory, which they were willing to defend, even from us. They had "wilded up" just four days from their release, barely seeming to recognize us. They had apparently been sleeping outside the release house, somewhere new: perhaps a lodge they were building, or that they had found but we couldn't see. Our release was a success and they were now wild beavers. It was exactly what rehabbers want to see when they release their charges back out into the wild.

I imagined this might be how parents would feel if they'd gone back four days after dropping their kid off at college to see their child thriving, making friends, attending all his or her classes. The child certainly would've reacted the way our beavers had: "What the hell are you doing here? Go home! Get out of my territory!" They would be glad their kid was having such a jolly time, but perhaps feel a small sting that they were not missed. If I felt this way, it was not the same as for a human child. I knew BK and Mrs. Beaver were wild, you see, and that I could never be a part of their world. For their own well-being, they had to become wary of humans again.

A month and a half later, on July 5, the day before my birthday, I saw BK and Mrs. Beaver for the last time. Laura and I traveled to the pond on Woodbury Mountain Road to dismantle and take away the release house, since the beavers should have found or built their own lodge by now. We found the house half dismantled, with the top flipped off, barely hanging on by its hinges, and the sides half undone, their screws sticking out. A young bull moose had come through the area just the day before, as recorded by the game camera we had set up on a nearby tree, and his tracks were fresh in the mud. It was clear the beavers had found other digs, since the house had ceased being habitable. I unscrewed what remained, barely holding the house together, and finally I freed the front part from the covered ramp going into the water. The house and ramp were now ready to be carried away, in pieces, from the pond, leaving behind barely a trace of our presence.

It was in the midst of doing all this that BK suddenly arrived and started coming up to me. I wasn't sure how wild he had become, so I kept him at bay with a small rake, and he ran into the water. Then Mrs. Beaver arrived and I had to keep her at bay with the rake too. Were they looking for apples or carrots? The two of them then started wrestling each other, perhaps reverting to their juvenile play in the presence of their parents. If possible, they looked even bigger than before; clearly they were not starving. I still didn't see their lodge anywhere; maybe it was out of our line of sight, in the far southwestern corner of the pond, behind the dam? As we carried out the last piece of the release house—the covered ramp—I looked back and had a last glimpse of BK. He was way out in the middle of the pond, swimming like a torpedo and leaving a V-shaped wave in his wake.

Goodbye BK. May the Beaver Gods bless you and keep you safe.

The Tragedy of Trapping

L ife went on after the release of our beavers. I continued to rehab birds and mammals. In fact, I had my busiest year to date in 2022, rescuing almost three dozen patients.

Perhaps the most amazing thing is that I took in another orphaned beaver kit not two weeks after I had released BK! My first thought was, "O God, I can't be going through all this again!" I really did not want to take in another beaver kit so soon after I had released BK. But wild animals in need of help wait for no man. In this case, like so many others, the cause of the animal's distress was man himself.

The baby beaver, whom we called Bubby, came in on June 1 from Jeffersonville, Vermont, and weighed in at 18.45 ounces, or just under one and a quarter pounds. She was even smaller than BK when I first got him and in fact was what Beaver Lady said kits weighed when they were newborn. Bubby couldn't have been more than a day or two old. Her parents had been trapped, out of season, by the caretaker of a property where a gravel road had washed out because its culvert had been dammed by the beavers. The owner wanted them dead. It was a problem that could've been easily solved by a Flow Device, as it later proved to be, installed by Mr. Beaver Deceiver. But for now I had to take care of trapping's casualty, this orphaned baby beaver.

At first everything went well. We fed and swam Bubby at least four times a day, feeding her with a syringe and the Miracle Nipple, so she drank on most days two batches of milk, or a half cup in total. She also did regular pees and poos when we swam her, either in the bathtub or outside in the garden pool. Bubby was quite active, either bounding around the bathroom floor, sniffing out our dirty under-wear and socks, or waddling across the lawn, going back and forth between Laura and me as we called to her by patting the ground. Bubby sheltered under my legs when she got scared, or fell asleep in the crook of my arm. I felt like I was becoming a beaver parent again, just like with BK. After about three weeks, Bubby weighed in at forty-five ounces, or just under three pounds, nearly triple her incoming weight.

Little did I know that this was to be the high point of Bubby's brief life. By the beginning of July, I began noticing she was losing weight. It was as if her body shut down, or simply decided to stop growing. Poor Bubby frequently had diarrhea, or else she emitted milky white poo, indicating the milk had passed through her body without anything being absorbed or converted into something else. She was also growing more listless, merely floating and not actively swimming in the pool, or sheltering under us and not exploring her surroundings on the lawn.

In the last ten days of Bubby's life, we made a last-ditch effort to save her. I called Beaver Lady and she advised me to treat her for a week with an antibiotic, Metronidazole, to cure any infection that might be in her gut, and at the same time give her some probiotics to restart her digestive bacteria or microbiome. Bubby seemed to rally once we started the treatment: Her poo became more tan or mustard-colored, which is what it should've been all along, and she started gaining weight again and becoming more lively. But then the diarrhea returned along with the milky whiteness of her poo.

On the twenty-fifth of July, Bubby died. Laura woke me at 6:30 A.M., telling me she was crashing. She was very lethargic, not even taking any milk or being able to swim when Laura put her in the bathtub. She put her down on a towel in her wooden house, and I watched her last death throes. At one point, she suddenly stood on her forepaws, as if she knew this was her time to die but wanted to simply walk away from Death. Then she thrashed her head from side to side in a jerky manner a couple of times. Finally, she lay still.

Later that morning, I took Bubby to our vet to have her autopsied. He found her last milk meal had gone undigested in a white ribbon throughout her digestive tract. He also saw that she had no os penis and was therefore a female. The vet concluded that Bubby hadn't gotten enough colostrum, or the first milk ingested by a newborn that is rich in antibodies and other "bioactives," which jumpstart the baby's immune system and seed the gut microbiome. Without it, as I saw firsthand, the newborn can't grow properly and stay healthy; there was nothing I could have done to save her. When Bubby's parents were trapped, she was also doomed. Only it took her a whole lot longer to die.

This horrible experience almost put me off rehab altogether. But that would mean Beaver Killer and all his trapper ilk had won. I determined to get more involved in the fight to ban trapping in Vermont.

The fact of the matter is, trapping is horribly cruel to wild animals, but especially to beavers. Trapping and hunting seasons are designed to avoid orphaning baby wild animals, or "young of the year."* This simply does not work

---

* The exception is coyotes, who can be hunted and shot all year round, 365 days of the year, in Vermont. This guarantees coyote pups will be orphaned every year. This speaks, of course, to the irrational hatred of coyotes in eastern states, similar to the rabid hatred of wolves out west.

for beavers, whose kits are dependent on their parents for *two* years. Therefore, trapping at any time of the year will orphan baby beavers and cause them to die without their parents. The question is, how many? If female beavers have three to four kits, on average, this means that for each colony, as many as eight kits born the previous two years could be present, and therefore thousands across Vermont could be orphaned and at risk every year.* No one really knows for sure, because no one has probed the lodges where colonies have been trapped for survivors, and the Vermont Department of Fish and Wildlife has no bag limits or any sort of regulations in terms of how many beavers may be trapped in any given location.** The trapping season for beavers in Vermont is incredibly long, stretching for nearly half the year, from the end of October until the end of March. Beaver kits orphaned at this time will die

---

* Based on a ten-year average, running from the trapping seasons of 2013-14 to 2023-24, 1174 beavers are trapped every year in Vermont, making them the second-most trapped animal in the state (behind muskrats). It is hard to know how many colonies this represents, but even if it is just a fourth (i.e., four beavers trapped from each colony), this would still mean that 2,348 kits are at risk every year. For trapping figures, see *Vermont Furbearer Management Newsletter* 20 (2024): 6.

** When I asked VDFW for information about specific sites where trappers had trapped beavers, they told me they did not have this information, as they only tracked trapping within broad "watershed management units" (Brehan Furfey, e-mail communication, February 16, 2024). Ultimately, I would have to get this information from trappers themselves. But how likely is it that they would give it to me?

from exposure to the cold, from starvation, or both. A similar conundrum arises for black bears, whose cubs stay with their parents for a year and a half (eighteen months) and therefore are likewise at risk of being orphaned two seasons in a row, during Vermont's nearly three-month-long bear hunting season (September 1–November 19).[*]

The trapping of nearly 1,200 beavers every year threatens hundreds of acres of prime wetland habitats. This runs directly counter to the stated mission of the VDFW, namely, "the conservation of fish, wildlife and plants and their habitats for the people of Vermont."[**] While it is true beavers often move on and abandon a site, so the wetland reverts to meadow and new tree growth, the beavers move

---

[*] In October 2022, a game camera mounted on the front porch of a resident in the Mad River Valley in central Vermont recorded a hunter shooting and killing a black bear sow as it was feeding under an apple tree with her two cubs. Three weeks later one of the cubs was found dead, starved to death, beside a nearby stream. The fate of the other cub is unknown. Based on the number of sows reported as killed by hunters, it is estimated 120 cubs are similarly orphaned every year in Vermont. On March 8, 2023, the resident presented a petition, based on extensive research, asking the VDFW Board to pass a regulation that would make the killing of a black bear sow in the presence of cubs illegal, instead of being merely a "recommendation" not to kill, and provide for hunter education to avoid such tragedies in the future. The VDFW Board unanimously rejected the petition.

[**] The VDFW's mission statement is given on the first page of its "Strategic Plan, 2022–2026," available online at vtfishandwildlife.com.

to a new site and create a new wetland. With trapping, that doesn't happen; the wetland is gone for good.

With so many beavers orphaned and so many existing and potential wetlands lost every year, how can the VDFW think trapping is good management policy for beavers or wildlife in general? After many hours researching this question, I came to the realization that the only way to make sense of it is to conclude that, like many fish and wildlife agencies across the country, VDFW is utterly beholden to the trapping/hunting community, a shrinking minority in Vermont that nonetheless maintains a stranglehold on wildlife management policy.[*] Indeed, VDFW will twist the facts, even outright lie to the public, in order to defend trapping. This is nothing less than a betrayal of the public trust, especially when the public gives great deference to the department as a supposedly unbiased scientific resource on wildlife. Instead, VDFW promotes trapping and hunting for entirely political reasons (i.e., to appease the trapping/hunting lobby), rather than any

---

[*] As of 2023, VDFW estimated there were 73,000 resident hunters in Vermont, 11 percent of the total population. The number of trappers is far smaller: As of 2022, VDFW counted 279 active trappers, i.e., those who submit annual reports of their kills, representing just 0.04 percent of the state's population. Altogether, 2,068 trapping licenses were reported as sold, on average, in a given year, representing 0.28 percent of the population. The Fish and Wildlife Board, which sets department policy, was at this time composed exclusively of hunters, trappers, and anglers.

scientific or biological imperative to conserve wildlife populations and their habitats.*

VDFW's main justification for trapping is that it is an allegedly effective means of population control and monitoring. However, there is absolutely no scientific evidence that this is true. The only "proof" I have ever seen for this claim is an outright lie.

In 1996, the state of Massachusetts passed by ballot referendum the Wildlife Protection Act, which banned the use of leghold and Conibear killing traps. In response, the Massachusetts Division of Fisheries and Wildlife (MassWildlife), which, like all state wildlife agencies, greatly resents the public "confounding" its management policies by voting on them, concocted a tale of Beaver Armageddon, in which beaver populations around the state allegedly exploded in the aftermath of the ban, because trappers could no longer trap and thereby control them. Correspondingly, nuisance complaints about beavers—that they were wreaking havoc with their damming activities by flooding roadways and other infrastructures—were also said to have exploded, thereby eroding human tolerance for wildlife and protection of

---

* In a 2018 *Media and Communications Survey*, 89 percent of respondents said being "caring about wildlife" described VDFW "very well" or "somewhat well." 69 percent said the same with regard to the department being "science based." However, a sizable percentage, 53 percent, described the department as being "influenced by politics."

their habitats, making the job of "professional" wildlife managers that much harder.*

But this cautionary tale of "Calamity by Design" is a complete fiction, dressed up in an imposing line and bar graph. A purple line ("known population growth") on the graph spikes upward by 50 percent in the year after the ban, while at the same time, the light blue bars underneath the line, designating the trapped harvest of beavers, shrink to almost nothing.** MassWildlife postulated a truly remarkable increase in beaver populations despite the fact that the database they used to track

---

* *Trapping and Furbearer Management in North American Wildlife Conservation*, 2nd ed. (2015), pp. 52–53, 55. One of the listed authors of this booklet is the Massachusetts Division of Fisheries and Wildlife.

** Here is the original graph, which is greatly modified on VDFW's online sidebar, "The Massachusetts Experience."

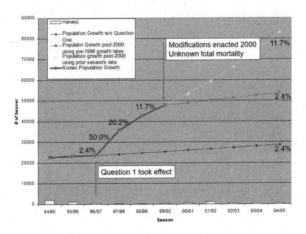

population trends—the reported trapped "harvest" of beavers—declined remarkably, going from 1,136 beavers just before the ban to just 98 the year after. How is this possible under any kind of statistical model?* When I asked this question of the MA state furbearer biologist, his answer was, "I am not familiar enough with the inner workings of the model to even speculate."** In other words, no one really knows what happened to beaver populations in Massachusetts after the ban.

Nevertheless, I've watched Vermont furbearer biologists trot out this graph in presentation after presentation about beavers as part of a scare tactic to allegedly show how trapping is the only thing standing between us and Beaver Armageddon. And Beaver Armageddon is not the only lie they tell. In one of their "Furbearer Management" newsletters, VDFW urged trappers to, "Post [on social media] tasteful photos, with as little blood and animal suffering as possible. We know animals in BMP [Best Management Practices] traps suffer

* The only possible scenario I can think of that might answer this question is that the *live trapping* of beavers increased by 50 percent after the ban. But since this was the only kind of trapping still allowed, it was being conducted in entirely different circumstances (i.e., by a great many more trappers) than before the ban.

** E-mail communication from Dave Wattles to John Aberth, April 1, 2021.

very little, but many people don't realize that."* This, too, is an outright lie. The Association of Fish and Wildlife Agencies (AFWA), which conducts trapping research on behalf of state agencies across the country, found in one study that up to 70 percent of animals caught in BMP leghold traps suffer "moderate" injuries and as much as 30 percent suffer "severe" ones. These injuries include: amputation of digits and limbs; tooth and bone fractures; deep tissue lacerations; internal organ damage; and even death.** In truth, wild animals can suffer for hours—exposed to the elements and predation—in leghold traps, which need only be checked by trappers once every twenty-four hours in Vermont. Beavers drown in specially set legholds attached to an underwater line that does not allow them to resurface once they dive into the water for safety after

---

* *Vermont Furbearer Management Newsletter*, 17 (2020): 7. On their current website, "Trappers and Dogs Sharing Trails," the VDFW states, "Foothold traps are designed to restrain an animal without harming them. . . . Pets caught in foothold traps can be easily released without harm." Yet this contradicts the research on BMP foothold traps conducted by the Association of Fish and Wildlife Agencies. See https://vtfishandwildlife.com, accessed January 17, 2025, and note below.

** H. Bryant White, et al., "Best Management Practices for Trapping Furbearers in the United States," *Wildlife Monographs*, December 2020.

being caught in the trap.* Since beavers are aquatic animals that can hold their breath for fifteen minutes, they take at least that long to die.**

Beavers, like all furbearers, do not need to have their populations "controlled" by humans. Instead, they self-regulate by suppressing their reproduction and dispersal in accordance with the *carrying capacity* of the land, or in other words, how much food and habitat is available to them. Beavers are very territorial and will not tolerate a *density* of more than two beaver colonies per stream mile (i.e., about

---

* Such "drown sets" are comprised of a leghold trap set in shallow water, attached by a chain to a wire line that is weighted to a deeper (at least 3 feet) part of the pond. When the beaver gets its paw caught in the trap, it panics and dives deeper into the water, unwittingly, to its death. The chain-line attachment does not allow the beaver to swim to the surface again. See attached illustration:

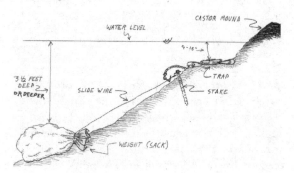

** Even Conibear "kill traps" kill animals instantaneously less than 15 percent of the time, so beavers usually also drown in such traps. See H.C. Lunn, *The Conibear Trap—Recommendations for its Improvement* (Humane Trap Development Committee of Canada, 1973).

ten beavers per stream mile). In fact, trapping beavers can stimulate their population growth by removing mature females and causing younger beavers to mature earlier, by as much as eight months, and stimulating them to have larger litters.* This is what seems to have happened in Massachusetts, when beaver populations doubled between 1993 and 1996, before the ban, when the state had a regular trapping season.** By contrast, areas that had no trapping (i.e., where it wasn't allowed) hosted beaver populations that followed a sigmoid, or S-shaped, pattern, meaning populations rose and fell over time. Usually beaver populations stabilized at well below carrying capacity all on their own. This has been demonstrated through on-the-ground colony count studies conducted over decades across the United States, including at Quabbin Reservoir in Massachusetts, Sagehen Creek in California, and Allegheny Park in New York.***

---

* H.E. Hodgdon, "Social Dynamics Within an Unexploited Beaver (Castor Canadensis) Population," (Ph.D. dissertation, University of Massachusetts, 1978), pp. 144–45.

** This population increase is *not* shown on the MassWildlife graph in footnote on p. 177, a rather convenient omission.

*** Peter E. Busher and Paul J. Lyons, "Long-Term Population Dynamics of the North American Beaver, *Castor canadensis*, on Quabbin Reservation, Massachusetts, and Sagehen Creek, California," in *Beaver Protection, Management, and Utilization in Europe and North America*, eds. Busher and Dzieciolowski (Plenum, 1999); D. Taylor, "Growth, Decline, and Equilibrium in a Beaver Population at Sagehen Creek, California" (Ph.D. dissertation, University of

California, Berkeley, 1970); personal communication from Sharon Brown to Massachusetts Society for the Prevention of Cruelty to Animals (MSPCA), 1998, as reported in MSPCA's online fact sheet, "The Beaver Population in Massachusetts: Myths and Facts," footnote 3, www.mspca.org/animal_protection/beaver-population, accessed January 27, 2024. The sigmoid pattern of beaver population movements in a natural environment without trapping is demonstrated in these two graphs of beaver colonies counted at Quabbin Reservoir from 1952 to 1996 and at Sagehen Creek from 1945 to 1991:

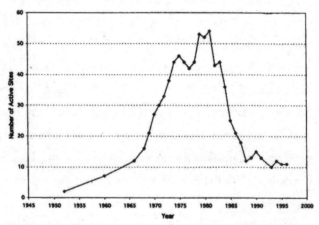

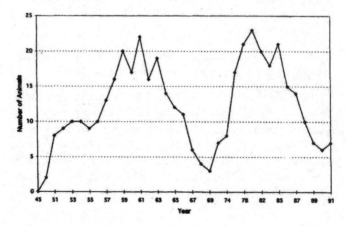

Beavers are far more valuable living on the landscape than hanging dead in a trapper's shed. Indeed, it could almost be considered a crime to trap beavers because removing them deprives the environment and all living things of the great and many benefits they provide.* I've already alluded, at the beginning of this book, to beavers being a "keystone" species for biodiversity by creating fantastic wetland habitats. But they provide so much more, such as improving water quality, storing water for times of drought, creating catchment areas to mitigate flooding, and acting as carbon sinks to combat climate change.** The water storage capacity of beaver ponds is truly impressive. For example, beaver ponds store five times as much water belowground as above, simply by slowing water flow so water can sink into the ground, and computer modeling has shown river basins without beavers

---

* Glynnis Hood, *The Beaver Manifesto* (Rocky Mountain Books, 2011).

** It is estimated that the combined value of beavers' "ecosystem services" amounts to $69,000 per square kilometer, or just over half a square mile, per year. In terms of carbon storage, active beaver ponds are estimated to store twelve to thirty-five times as much carbon as grasslands, which typically succeed beaver-maintained wetlands once beavers are removed from the site. See: S. Thompson, M. Vehkaoja, J. Pellikka, and P. Nummi, "Ecosystem Services Provided by Beavers *Castor* spp.," *Mammal Review* 51 (2021): 25–39; E. Wohl, "Landscape-scale Carbon Storage Associated with Beaver Dams," *Geophysical Research Letters* 40 (2013): 3631–36; Chris E. Jordan and Emily Fairfax, "Beaver: The North American Freshwater Climate Action Plan," *WIREsWATER* 9 (2022): e1592.

can increase their water storage capacity by as much as nine times, worth billions of dollars, by allowing thousands of beavers to move in.* Everyone benefits from live beavers working for us on the landscape; the only limit to beavers' natural productivity potential is our tolerance for them.** Other furbearers, including coyotes, foxes, bobcats, fishers, and mink, have proven their worth in controlling prey species, such as deer and mice, that pose issues for humans, such as overbrowsing

---

* This is based on research conducted in eastern Washington state and in the Milwaukee River watershed in Wisconsin. The Milwaukee River study found its watershed could potentially accommodate 4,563 beavers, whose dam-building activities would provide storage for 1.7 billion gallons of water annually, worth $3.3 billion. See: Ben Goldfarb, *Eager: The Surprising, Secret Life of Beavers and Why They Matter*, repr. edn. (Chelsea, VT: Chelsea Green Publishing, 2019); Qian Liao, et al., *Project: Hydrological Impact of Beaver Habitat Restoration in the Milwaukee River Watershed*, November 2020.

** Professional wildlife managers call this human tolerance for wildlife the *social carrying capacity*, which they use to justify trapping by claiming the number of beavers allowed to live on the landscape must be lower than the actual carrying capacity to avoid beavers making a nuisance of themselves with their human neighbors. But social carrying capacity is also just as much a function of education, i.e., informing the public as to why beavers are such a valuable resource, and making them aware of nonlethal solutions that are far more sustainable than trapping.

vegetation, colliding with cars, or being reservoirs of Lyme disease.*

There is one further consideration for why trapping is detrimental to good wildlife management. The open-faced jaws of a leghold, and even of a Conibear, trap are, as you might expect, highly indiscriminate of whatever paw or other appendage might trigger the trip pan that snaps them mercilessly shut. Trappers have testified that they typically trap and kill two non-target animals for every target captured.** This means state wildlife agencies cannot "fine-tune" trapping culls based on the age, sex, health, or even a specific species to be targeted,

---

* Much of the research on furbearers' impact on Lyme disease has been conducted by the Cary Institute (CI) of Ecosystem Studies in Dutchess County, NY, and is available on their website: www .caryinstitute.org/topics/lyme-disease, accessed December 27, 2023. The CI found the mere presence of predators like foxes could help reduce the incidence of Lyme, simply by keeping mice that carry the *Borrelia bergdorferi* bacteria in their blood cowering in their holes, rather than aboveground where they can infect tick vectors that feed on them.

** D. Randall, *Hearings before the Ninety-Fourth Congress to Discourage the Use of Painful Devices in the Trapping of Animals and Birds* (U.S. Government Printing Office, 1975); M. Novak, "The Foot-Snare and the Leg-Hold Traps: A Comparison," *Proceeding of the Worldwide Furbearer Conference* 3 (1981): 1671–85; M. Novak, "Traps and Trap Research," in *Wild Furbearer Management and Conservation in North America*, eds. M. Novak, J.A. Baker, M.E. Obbard, and B. Malloch (Ontario Trappers Association, 1987), pp. 941–69.

as is typically done for hunting. Although the VDFW claims BMP traps are "highly selective," this, too, is a demonstrable lie. The result of AFWA's field-testing of BMP traps is that these are selective merely of the entire furbearer species that can legally be targeted by trappers, as opposed to, say, the (unintentional) trapping of endangered species (by definition few and far between!).* The only possible advantage of trapping is that it supplies indiscriminately sourced samples for biological testing; however, such samples can just as easily be sourced from roadkill, scat piles, and fur snags, without subjecting the animals to horrendous suffering and death.

Even if we leave beavers alone to expand and contract their populations in accordance with their natural cycles, there will still be times and places where they expand into human population centers and thereby make a "nuisance" of themselves. They may do this, say, by damming culverts—which, to a beaver, is simply a hole in a massive dam, the roadway, that instinct commands must be plugged—causing flooding to man-made infrastructure that, from a beaver's perspective, was never meant to be there. This is indeed another way fish and wildlife departments justify trapping, allegedly as a way to help

---

* *Vermont Furbearer Management Newsletter* 17 (2020): 1; White, et al., "Best Management Practices for Trapping."

prevent such conflicts. But trappers only respond to nuisance complaints after the fact, not before, and they often recreationally trap in places away from population centers with little to no infrastructure, such as Wildlife Management Areas (WMAs), and in not nearly enough numbers to realistically make a difference in terms of avoiding conflicts.

Whether the problem be beavers flooding our roadways or black bears rooting through our garbage, we will never be able to kill our way to solving these conflicts. Indeed, it is manifestly unfair to punish animals with the ultimate penalty—death—simply for following their natural instinct to survive. If humans truly are the most intelligent, the most noble, the most civilized of creatures, then it is incumbent upon us to find a way to resolve the quarrels we have with our beastly neighbors without resorting to our basest instincts—namely, by committing violence and meting out death.

Because beavers are aquatic animals, our relationship with them is complicated. With climate change, we are discovering the roads and homes we built in floodplains after beavers were all trapped in the eighteenth and nineteenth centuries were never meant to be there, but really belong to the beavers. Beavers are the only ones who can tame floods by creating catchment areas with their dams, even if we are now trying to imitate them

by deliberately felling trees in the river's path.* But
when dams are perceived as creating the flooding itself,
beavers are blamed.

Most nuisance trapping of beavers is done under the
auspices of town road crews and state transportation agencies charged with the maintenance of our highways and
byways. Too often, town road crew foremen are "old
school" when it comes to addressing beaver nuisance
complaints; almost by default, they quickly resort to
killing the beavers, either by trapping or simply shooting
them, which is done by removing a part of the dam (an
illegal act) so the sound of flowing water draws out
the beavers. The Vermont Agency of Transportation
(VTrans) also traps and kills a lot of beavers. VTrans's
trappers are known to go out in the early morning hours,
when beavers are most active but also when no one is
looking, and trap beavers before any commuters have to
see this unpleasant sight on their way to work. VTrans
will also trap beavers before they even finish their dams in
an attempt to be "proactive" about any damage it is imagined the beavers might cause. VTrans claims it must take

---

* This is known as Strategic Wood Addition (SWA) and is a strategy
often used to improve fish habitat. See VDFW's website, "Strategic
Wood Addition to Improve Stream Habitat," at vtfishandwildlife.
com/conserve/aquatic-habitat-conservation/strategic-wood-addition
-to-improve-stream-habitat, accessed February 24, 2024.

these measures "in order to protect the safety of travelers on our roads before all else," but sometimes I have seen beavers killed and dams removed even though the beaver dams were situated in such a way that they were keeping water back *away* from the road, and were thereby protecting it and its travelers *from* flooding!

Finally, private landowners are allowed to trap, shoot, and kill beavers and other furbearers at any time of the year to protect their properties from "damage." The vague and overly permissive language of Vermont statutes means private landowners or their hired Nuisance Wildlife Control Officers (NWCO) can, like VTrans, kill any furbearing animal even *before* they've caused any damage at all, on the dubious assumption that they are threatening to do so by their mere presence. How many animals are killed by such means is not known since landowners are not even required to report their activities.

In truth, no beaver has to be killed, ever, to resolve a nuisance complaint. That's because Mr. Beaver Deceiver invented Flow Devices (FDs) to protect culverts and lower pond levels behind dams. These have been proven to be effective, beyond their first or second year, 87–97 percent of the time. If they do fail, it is usually because of a lack of maintenance in clearing woody debris built up around the device. By contrast, trapping *fails* 84 percent of the time, meaning that beavers are back within one or two years

of a colony being trapped out of a site.* Because FDs last
so long, typically twenty to thirty years, they are also far
more cost-effective than trapping, since little has to be
spent beyond the initial investment of installing the device.
This is why FDs are typically half as expensive, per annum,
compared to trapping every year.**

We clearly have the means, and the motive, to save
beavers. All that seems to be lacking is the will. I have
gone to many towns around Vermont to consult with, or
say my piece about, beavers and why we shouldn't be trapping them. Some town Selectboards—typically three to
five men or women elected to serve as the executive arm
of local government—have been receptive. Others have

---

* This is based on a client survey conducted by Beaver Solutions of
Southampton, MA, presented in the following table:

Management Method	Total Sites	Total Successful	Total Failed	Failed <1 Yr	Failed 1-2 Yrs	Failed >2 Yrs
Culvert Devices	227	220 (97%)	7 (3%)	5	2	0
Pond Levelers	156	135 (87%)	21 (13%)	21	0	0
Cylindrical Fences	30	18 (60%)	12 (40%)	9	0	3
Trapping Only	69	8 (16%)	43 (84%)	3	34	6
Total	482					

** A survey conducted by Beaver Solutions of fifty-five "conflict sites"
managed at Billerica, MA, between 2000 and 2019, with forty-three
sites managed nonlethally using FDs and twelve "no tolerance" sites
managed every year by trapping, concluded the average annual-
ized cost of the former was just $229, versus $409 for the latter. See
Michael Callahan, Richard Berube, and Isabel Tourkantonis, "Billerica Municipal Beaver Management Program: 2000–2019 Analysis,"
unpublished paper.

shouted me down or simply refused to let me speak, or to really hear what I have to say. Often, VDFW stymies my efforts. Although the department has a FD program of its own (which it calls the "Beaver Wetlands Conservation Project"), this pays mere lip service to its obligated Best Management Practices for beaver. The program is underfunded, resulting in low-quality outdated devices (i.e., a simple exclusion fence around the culvert) that often fail within the first year or two. In such cases, it almost would have been better to build no device at all, because trappers feel justified and emboldened to trap again once a device fails. Too often, game wardens and department biologists tell towns and property owners to trap or shoot beavers as a first resort or as the town's only option because FDs are not viable.* The attraction of simply killing the beavers is that it is quickly implemented (I would also call it lazy), while installing a high-quality FD takes longer and requires more planning and expertise. But in the long term, trapping is not sustainable. As more towns have successes with FDs and incorporate nonlethal approaches into their strategic plans, this convinces other towns to do the same.

---

* By contrast, Mr. Beaver Deceiver, who was responsible for implementing VDFW's FD program at its very inception, has told me, "There's not a [beaver] conflict site that I can't eliminate non-lethally." Skip Lisle, e-mail communication, November 13, 2020.

Once upon a time, beavers ruled this land.* It is said that, before white settlers, there were four hundred million of them in North America, or sixty-seven beavers per square mile. This is wildly unrealistic; at most, the continent could support sixty million beavers, which would still mean their current numbers of six to twelve million are only a fraction, or roughly a fifth, of what they once were.** This is like what happened to American bison, the buffalo, which numbered thirty to sixty million prior to the nineteenth century. Tragically, this keystone species of the grassland prairie was slaughtered in their millions, particularly in the 1870s, when, not coincidentally, it was US government policy to exterminate Indigenous people from their homelands. Could it ever be possible that,

---

* See Leila Philip, *Beaverland: How One Weird Rodent Made America* (New York: Twelve Books, 2022). In my opinion, this book is far too indulgent of trapping, especially evident in chapters 4 and 5. Trappers are portrayed here as the last frontiersmen living off the land, but the other side of the coin, the viewpoint of "antis" who are opposed to trapping, is never presented.

** I am inclined to sixty million, at the low end of pre-European population estimates, because beavers are so very territorial, allowing at most two beaver colonies—or roughly ten individuals—per stream mile. In the United States, it is estimated that there are roughly 3.6 million miles of rivers and streams, which would allow for 36 million beavers. See Hodgdon, "Social Dynamics," pp. 135–37; US EPA Archive Document, Appendix A-1: "Total Miles of Rivers and Streams in the Nation," available online at https://archive.epa.gov, accessed February 23, 2025.

somehow, we get back to something of the demographic splendor beavers and bison once enjoyed?

We can never entirely erase the footprint of our settlements that encroached upon beavers' home ranges in the first place. But if we are to have even a chance of atoning for our original sin of slaughter and destruction, we must end trapping. Only by ending extraneous killing can we allow beavers to reclaim their rightful habitats and expand to their full demographic potential, thereby maximizing their many benefits, both to other animals and to us. There is room to expand, just like there is room for bison out west. For me, personally, this is also a chance to exponentialize my advocacy for wild animals. I may be able to save a few individuals a year by rehab, but I could potentially save hundreds, if not thousands, of beavers by campaigning against trapping.

As I leave you, to hopefully fight your own battles on behalf of wildlife, I offer the following six principles—which I call the "Aberth Manifesto"—as perhaps a way we can peacefully coexist with wild animals and thereby fight the biodiversity crisis and extinction events threatening wildlife around the globe.

It is dedicated to BK.

THE ABERTH MANIFESTO

Six Ways to Coexist with Wild Animals

1. Laws that protect against cruelty to animals should apply to all animals, including wild animals.

2. Wild animals deserve half, or 50 percent, of all land set aside as their natural habitat (with migration corridors a priority).

3. Only nonlethal methods should be used to resolve "nuisance" or conflict situations between humans and wild animals. To kill an animal is to unfairly punish an animal for simply trying to survive, and an admission of failure of supposedly superior human intelligence.

4. Hunting of wild animals must accord with the rules of "fair chase" and a "clean kill." Trapping is not the same as hunting and causes undue suffering. Animals should not be hunted as "trophies" or poached for totemic body parts.

5. Our pursuit of commercial farming and fishing must not come at the expense of the welfare and survival of wild animals. No animal predator should be killed that is seen as competing with us as human predators (hunters).

6. All wild animals play a role in the earth's ecosystem and thus have value. To demonize an animal is to define it solely in terms of human understanding, not as an integral part of the "web of life" whose interconnections lie beyond our ken.

Acknowledgments

I would like to acknowledge the following individuals for their help at various stages in the rehabilitation process for beavers and other animals: Josh Gray, who found BK and brought him to me to be rehabbed; Cher Button-Dobmeier, of the Abbe-Freeland Animal Sanctuary, for her invaluable expertise and advice on rehabbing beavers; Skip Lisle of Beaver Deceivers International, for his invaluable expertise and advice on beaver habitat; Leroy Hadden, DVM, of Valley Animal Hospital, for his veterinary services to beavers; Dan Hament, DVM, of Richmond Animal Hospital, for his veterinary services to raptors; Tom Stuwe, DVM, and his assistant, Laura Milne, for x-ray services on beavers; Heidi Albright and her family, of Third Branch Flower, for providing all the willow and poplar sticks that fed the beavers; Brenna Galdenzi, of Protect Our Wildlife, for material and emotional support; Tina Fitts and her family, Scott Hamilton and his family, and Terry Romero and her family, for supporting all our endeavors on the farm; and David Kelley, of Vermont Wildlife Coalition, for his legal advice.

Above all, I must thank my wife, Laura Hamilton, for being a rehabilitation partner and co-parent to BK.

Wildlife rehab is an expensive endeavor that is done on a strictly volunteer basis. Without the love and support of all the above, it simply would not be possible.

Truly, it takes a village to raise a beaver!

Index

A

"Aberth Manifesto," 193, 194–195

A/D pet food, 59, 62–63, 67, 120–121

Albright, Heidi, 28, 125, 160, 196

Allegheny Park, 181

animals

  coexisting with, 193, 194–195

  cruelty to, 3, 8, 41–42, 86, 169–195

  ecosystems and, 3–4, 183–185, 195

  hunting, 172, 174–175, 185–186, 195

  nonlethal solutions, 184, 190–191, 194

  rehabbing, 1–23, 25–43, 45–67, 69–95, 97–160, 165, 169–172

  role of, 3–4, 183–184, 195

  trapping, 8, 41–42, 86, 115, 132–137, 169–193, 195

antibiotics, 76, 81–83, 86, 101, 116, 127, 140, 171

anti-inflammatory steroids, 127, 129

Association of Fish and Wildlife Agencies (AFWA), 179, 186

Aulds Cove, Nova Scotia, 34

B

Baby Weasel, 120–126

Barre, Vermont, 61

barred owl, 19, 66–67, 139

Baytril, 81–82, 127

Bean (beaver), 70, 86–87

bears, 102, 174, 187

Beaver, Miss, 70, 80–87, 116–120, 138, 141, 150

Beaver, Mrs., 70, 85–120, 131, 139–146, 148, 153, 157–167

Beaver Armageddon, 176, 178

Beaver Baffle, 149

Beaver Dam Analog (BDA), 149–151

Beaver Deceiver, Mr. (Skip), 149–151, 170, 189, 191

Beaver Killer, 135–136, 172

Beaver Lady (Cher), 4–6, 8, 12, 41, 76, 87, 93–95, 101, 150, 157–158, 170–171

Beaver Manifesto, The, 183

"Beaver Population in Massachusetts: Myths and Facts," 182

Beaver Protection, Management, and Utilization in Europe and North America, 181

Beaver Solutions, 190

"Beaver: The North American Freshwater Climate Action Plan," 183

"Beaver Wetlands Conservation Project," 191

Beaverettes, 69–70, 80, 84–85, 87

Beaverland: How One Weird Rodent Made America, 192

beavers

  in basement, 45–57, 131–146

  in bathtub, 7–18

  building dams, 31–32, 37–38, 46, 84, 111–113, 148–153, 157, 184, 186–189

  building lodges, 84, 86, 111, 113, 138–139, 148–149, 153, 165–167

  carrying capacity for, 180–181, 184

  colonies of, 3, 5, 41, 70, 148, 153, 173, 180–181

  colonies per stream mile, 148, 180–181, 192

  diet for, 8–12, 27–28, 36–37, 54, 74, 82–84, 90–92, 100, 103, 106, 110–111, 131, 144–145, 159–162, 164–165

  ecosystems and, 3–4, 183–184, 195

  enclosures for, 18, 25, 45–48, 51–57, 72–75, 77–78, 80–83, 87–95, 101–120, 132–145, 148, 151, 153, 158–160

  evacuating, 105, 108–109

  first feeding of, 8–9

  first winter for, 40–43, 45–67

  fur trade and, 8, 14, 51

  habitats for, 3–4, 32, 174–177, 180, 183–184, 191, 193

  injuries to, 80–85, 100, 116–119, 179–180

  leaving colony, 5, 41–42, 70, 81, 153

  litters of, 71–72, 84–85, 150, 173, 181

  mating games for, 69–95

  orphaned beavers, 2–3, 5–8, 35, 41–42, 70–71, 85–86, 135, 169–175

populations of, 173, 176–178, 181–182, 192
post release, 164–167, 169
rehabbing, 4–18, 25–43, 45–57, 69–95, 97–120, 131–167, 169–172
release day for, 160–163
release house for, 157–162, 164–167
release site for, 147–157
releasing into wild, 147–167
second winter for, 131–146
stream time for, 30–39, 40–41, 102–115, 118, 158–160
survival rates of, 5–6, 41–42, 172–174
swimming tank for, 10–13, 25–27, 30–31, 36, 42, 51–57, 69, 72–75, 77–78, 81–82, 85, 88–94, 97–102, 105–108, 110–111, 131, 140–146, 153, 163
trapping, 8, 41–42, 86, 114, 132–136, 170, 172–195
walking with, 30–31, 35, 37–43
weight concerns for, 7, 73, 81, 88, 169–171
weight gains for, 18, 50, 73, 81 108, 145, 153, 170–171
wrestling games of, 33–35, 48–51, 54–57, 71–72, 78–79, 98–99, 103–104, 106, 146, 163
See also specific beavers
Benson, Vermont, 70
Berube, Richard, 190
"Best Management Practices for Trapping Furbearers in the United States," 179, 186
Betadine, 81–83, 117
"Billerica Municipal Beaver Management Program: 2000–2019 Analysis," 190
bison, 192–193
BK (Beaver Kit), 7–18, 23, 25–43, 45–57, 69–84, 87–95, 97–132, 139–146, 148, 151–153, 157–167, 169–170, 193
black bears, 102, 174, 187
bobcats, 102, 184
Brown, Sharon, 182
Bubby, 169–172
Buddha pose, 13, 48
buffalo, 192–193
Bugs (Lovebug), 39, 43

Busher, Peter E., 181
Button-Dobmeier, Cher, 4–6, 12, 41, 76, 87, 93–95, 101, 149–150, 157–158, 171, 196

C
Calais, Vermont, 161
Callahan, Michael, 190
Canso Causeway, 34
Cape Breton Island, 34
carrying capacity, 180–181, 184
Cary Institute (CI) of Ecosystem Studies, 185
Catholic Church, 14, 51
Chipmunk, Mr., 35–37, 46
"Climate Change Superheroes," 4
coexistence with wild animals, 193–195
Colchester, Vermont, 139
colonies
 close bonds within, 5–6, 173
 forming own, 153, 156
 graphs of, 182
 leaving, 5, 41–42, 70, 81, 153, 173
 number of, 173, 180–182, 192
 per stream mile, 148, 180–181, 192
 return of, 189–190, 193
 survivors of, 2–3, 173
Conibear Trap—Recommendations for its Improvement, 180
Connecticut River, 31
Convenia, 83, 116, 140
Cooper's hawk, 126–129
coprophagia, 9–10
Coronavirus pandemic, 2, 15, 61
coyotes, 152, 172, 184
crows, 20
cruelty to animals, 3, 8, 41–42, 86, 149, 169–195
culverts
 dams and, 149–150, 170, 186, 189, 191
 Flow Device for, 149–150, 170, 189–191
 protecting, 149–150, 170, 189, 191

D
dams
 beavers building, 31–32, 37–38, 46, 84, 111–113, 148–153, 157, 184, 186–187
 crushing, 2–3, 36, 188

culverts and, 149–150, 170, 186, 189, 191
damming instincts, 150, 186–187
existing dams, 152, 157, 162, 164, 167
starter dams, 149–151
deer, 2–3, 184
diets
A/D pet food, 59, 62–63, 67, 120–121
apples, 74, 82–84, 91, 98, 111, 144–145, 164–165
carrots, 82–84, 91, 111, 144, 162, 164–165
chicken breast, 59–60
earthworms, 127
kale, 98
mice, 19–22, 59–60, 63–65, 67, 121–126, 128–130
milk formulas, 8–12, 27–28, 120–121, 170–172
Rodent Chow nuggets, 9, 17, 27–28, 31, 35–37, 54, 84, 90, 100, 103, 106, 109–110, 144–145, 159, 162, 164
water lilies/pondweed, 145
weight concerns and, 7, 73, 81, 88, 169–171
weight gains and, 18, 50, 108, 145, 153, 170–171
willow/poplar sticks, 9, 13, 27–28, 82, 84, 90, 94, 103, 106, 131, 145, 159–162
"discharges," 113, 115, 132–134, 137
Dogloo, 25, 28–30, 37, 39–42, 46, 81–82, 84–85, 102–103, 105, 109, 113
Duxbury, Vermont, 127

E
Eager: The Surprising, Secret Life of Beavers and Why They Matter, 184
"Ecosystem Services Provided by Beavers Castor," 183
ecosystems, 3–4, 183–184, 195. See also habitats
Emaciation Protocol, 57–58, 67
Emeraid protein powder, 58–60, 67
enclosures
in basement, 45–57, 131–146
for beavers, 18, 25, 45–48, 51–57, 72–75, 77–78, 80–83, 87–95, 101–120, 132–145, 148, 151, 153, 158–160
hoisting, 132, 137–138, 158

moving, 104, 106, 115
prohibiting, 113–116, 132–138
evacuations, 105, 108–109

F
Fairfax, Emily, 183
falconry, 19, 66, 129
falcons, 1, 126, 129–130
Fayston, Vermont, 65, 67
Fish Hatchery, 114–115
Flint Brook, 31–33, 118, 133
Flow Devices (FDs), 149–150, 170, 189–191
Flower Girl (Heidi), 28, 125, 160, 196
"Foot-Snare and the Leg-Hold Traps: A Comparison," 185
foxes, 184
Freedom of Information Act (FOIA), 134–135
Frog, Mrs., 13
fur trade, 8, 14, 51
"Furbearer Management," 178
Furfey, Brehan, 173

G
Gray, Josh, 1–2, 4, 196
Geophysical Research Letters, 183
Goldfarb, Ben, 184
great blue heron, 130
"Growth, Decline, and Equilibrium in a Beaver Population at Sagehen Creek, California," 181

H
habitats
beaver habitats, 3–4, 32, 174–177, 180, 183–184, 191, 193
ecosystems and, 3–4, 183–184, 195
fields, 22
fish habitat, 32, 188
forests, 22
owl habitats, 22, 57
preserving, 188, 194
streams, 188
tundra, 57
wetlands, 3–4, 174–177, 180, 183–184, 191
Hamilton, Laura, 1, 4–13, 15–17, 19, 22–23, 25–26, 29–40, 42–43, 45,

49–55, 62, 65, 67, 71–84, 87, 89,
   91–94, 97–98, 100–118, 120–122,
   131–132, 137, 141, 143, 145,
   148–152, 156, 158–162, 164–166,
   170–171, 196
Hardwick, Vermont, 154
Havahart trap, 21, 64, 122–123
hawks, 1, 4, 126–129, 152
*Hearings before the Ninety-Fourth
   Congress to Discourage the Use of
   Painful Devices in the Trapping of
   Animals and Birds*, 185
heron, 130
Hinesburg, Vermont, 21–22
Hodgdon, H. E., 181, 192
Hood, Glynnis, 183
hunting, 172, 174–175, 186, 195

I

Imprinting protocol, 20, 73, 81, 108,
   145, 153, 170–17121
injuries
   to beavers, 80–85, 100–101, 116–119,
      179–180
   to hawk, 127–129
   to merlin, 129–130
   to woodcock, 126–127
Intensive Care Ward, 58, 60, 80, 127–128
Inverness, Nova Scotia, 34
Irasburg, Vermont, 57
Ivermectin, 59

J

Jeffersonville, Vermont, 169
Jelly, 70, 86–87, 94, 101, 113. *See also*
   Beaver, Mrs.
Jordan, Chris E., 183

L

"Landscape-scale Carbon Storage
   Associated with Beaver Dams," 183
Liao, Qian, 184
Lisle, Skip, 149–151, 170, 189, 191
litters, 71–72, 84, 150, 173, 181
live prey test, 21, 64, 122–125, 128–129
lodges
   beavers building, 84, 86, 111, 113,
      138–139, 148–149, 165, 167
   crushing, 2–3, 36

shape of, 28
warmth of, 41, 48, 51, 86
long-eared owl, 18–23, 25
"Long-Term Population Dynamics of
   the North American Beaver, *Castor
   canadensis*, on Quabbin Reservation,
   Massachusetts, and Sagehen Creek,
   California," 181
Lunn, H. C., 180
Lyme disease, 185
Lyons, Paul J., 181

M

Mad River Valley, 174
Mammal Review, 183
Massachusetts Division of Fisheries and
   Wildlife, 176–178, 181
"Massachusetts Experience, The," 177
Massachusetts Society for the Prevention
   of Cruelty to Animals (MSPCA),
   182
Mating Game, 69–95
Mazuri, 28, 84, 90, 162
Media and Communications Survey, 176
merlins, 126, 129–130
Metacam, 127, 129
Metronidazole, 171
mice, 19–22, 59–60, 63–65, 67, 121–126,
   128–130, 184–185
Middlebury, Vermont, 18
migration corridors, 194
mink, 2–3, 7, 61–65, 67, 184
Missing Link supplement, 120–121
Monkton, Vermont, 152–153
Montpelier, Vermont, 81, 154, 161
moose, 3, 166
Mud Pond, 154–156
muskrats, 173

N

nature preserve, 147, 154
nonlethal solutions, 184, 190–191, 194.
   See also Flow Devices
Northeast Kingdom, Vermont, 57
Northeast Wilderness Trust (NEWT),
   147, 154, 161–162
northern flicker, 130
Notice of Alleged Violation (NOAV),
   133–134, 137

Novak, M., 185
Nuisance Wildlife Control Officers
    (NWCO), 189
Nummi, P., 183

O
Old Vermonter, 154–156
Oreo (rabbit), 42, 45, 57
orphans
  bears, 174
  beavers, 2–7, 35, 41–42, 70–71, 85–86,
    169–175
  owls, 18–19
  weasels, 120
owls
  barred owl, 19, 66–67, 139
  habitats for, 22, 57
  long-eared owl, 18–23, 25
  rehabbing, 1, 18–23, 57–61, 64–67,
    139
  releasing into wild, 22–23, 25, 67
  snowy owl, 57–61, 64, 67

P
Pellikka, J., 183
Philip, Leila, 192
pigeon hawks, 129. See also merlins
poaching, 195
post release, 164–167, 169
Proceeding of the Worldwide Furbearer
    Conference 185
Project: Hydrological Impact of Beaver
    Habitat Restoration in the Milwaukee
    River Watershed, 184
Protect Our Wildlife (POW), 106, 115,
    134–135, 154, 196
Pumpkin (beaver), 70–79, 88, 116,
    118–120, 138–139, 150

Q
Quabbin Reservoir, 181–182

R
rabbit, 42, 45, 57
Randall, D., 185
Randolph, Vermont, 129–130
raptors, 1–2, 19–20
rats, 1, 3
ravens, 20

rehabbing
  beavers, 4–18, 25–43, 45–57, 69–95,
    97–120, 131–167, 169–172
  hawks, 1, 4, 126–129
  merlin, 126, 129–130
  mink, 61–65
  owls, 1, 18–23, 57–67, 139
  weasel, 120–126
  woodcock, 126–127
releases
  beaver release day, 160–163
  beaver release house, 157–167
  beaver release site, 147–157
  beavers post release, 164–167, 169
  of hawk, 129
  of merlin, 130
  of mink, 64–65
  of owls, 22–23, 25, 67
  of weasel, 125–126
  of woodcock, 127
reservoirs, 181–182
Rodent Chow nuggets, 9, 17, 27–28,
    31, 35–37, 54, 84, 90, 100, 103,
    106, 109–110, 144–145, 159, 162,
    164
Roxbury, Vermont, 115, 135, 151

S
Sagehen Creek, 181–182
St. Albans, Vermont, 1, 36
snowy owl, 57–61, 64, 67
social carrying capacity, 184
"Social Dynamics Within an
    Unexploited Beaver (Castor
    Canadensis) Population," 181, 192
Social Services, 114–115
Statute 1259a, 113, 115, 133, 135–137
Stowe, Vermont, 70, 80–81
"Strategic Plan, 2022–2026" (VDFW),
    174
Strategic Wood Addition (SWA), 188
"Strategic Wood Addition to Improve
    Stream Habitat," 188
stream time, 30–39, 40–41, 102–115,
    118, 158–160
subQ (subcutaneous) fluids, 58, 130
survival rates, 5–6, 41, 172–174
swimming tanks, 10–13, 25–27, 30–31,
    36, 42, 51–57, 69, 72–75, 77–78,

81–82, 85, 88–94, 97–102, 105–108,
   110–111, 131, 140–146, 153, 163
Swimming-in-Place, 56, 78–80
Swimway, 33–34, 37–39, 103, 111

T

Taylor, D., 181
Thompson, S., 183
timberdoodle, 126–127
"Total Miles of Rivers and Streams in
   the Nation," 192
Tourkantonis, Isabel, 190
Trail Around Middlebury (TAM), 18
trappers, 86, 114–115, 134–137, 146,
   170, 172–193, 195
"Trappers and Dogs Sharing Trails," 179
trapping
   beavers, 8, 41–42, 51, 86, 114–115,
      132–136, 170, 172–193, 195
   BMP traps, 178–179, 186
   Conibear traps, 176, 180, 185
   cruelty of, 8, 41–42, 86, 170–193, 195
   "drown sets," 180
   laws regarding, 134, 136–137, 195
   leghold traps, 176, 179–180, 185–186
   licenses, 134, 175
   research on, 175–182, 185–186
   trapping season, 41–42, 135, 170,
      172–173, 181
   types of traps, 115, 132–136, 176,
      179–180, 185–186
   underwater traps, 115, 132–136, 180
*Trapping and Furbearer Management
   in North American Wildlife
   Conservation*, 177
"Traps and Trap Research," 185
Tropical Storm Fred, 109
Trout, Mr., 32–33

V

Vehkaoja, M., 183
Vermont Agency of Transportation
   (VTrans), 188–189
Vermont Department of Environmental
   Conservation (DEC), 113–116, 120,
   132–134,

Vermont Department of Fish and
   Wildlife (VDFW), 2, 61, 85–86,
   133–134, 136, 173–179, 186, 188,
   191
*Vermont Furbearer Management
   Newsletter*, 173, 179, 186
Vermont Gazetteer, 155
Vermont Wildlife Coalition (VWC),
   134, 136
Vetericyn, 101

W

Waitsfield, Vermont, 139
walking with beaver, 30–31, 35, 37–43
watershed management units, 173
watershed study, 184
Wattles, Dave, 178
weasels, 2, 120–126
weight concerns, 7, 73, 81, 88, 169–171
weight gains, 18, 50, 73, 81, 108, 145,
   153, 170–171
wetland habitats, 3–4, 174–177, 180,
   183–184, 191
White, H. Bryant, 179, 186
White River, 31
*Wild Furbearer Management and
   Conservation in North America*, 185
Wildlife Management Areas (WMAs),
   187
Wildlife Monographs, 179
Wildlife Protection Act (MA), 176
wildlife rehabilitation, 1–23, 25–43,
   45–67, 69–95, 97–167, 169–172, 193
Williamstown, Vermont, 129
WIREsWATER, 183
Wohl, E., 183
Wolcott, Vermont, 120
wolves, 172
Woodbury, Vermont, 147, 154, 161
Woodbury Mountain Wilderness
   Preserve, 147, 154
woodcock, 126–127
woodpecker, 130
wrestling games, 33–35, 48–51, 54–57,
   71–72, 78–79, 98–99, 103–104, 106,
   146, 163